D0700005

To Ron Tobin

for the sake of auld lang syne

Roy

x, 91

CORNEILLE'S TRAGEDIES
The Role of the Unexpected

CORNEILLE'S TRAGEDIES

The Role of the Unexpected

R.C. KNIGHT

CARDIFF
UNIVERSITY OF WALES PRESS
1991

British Library Cataloguing in Publication Data

Knight, R.C. (Roy Clement)
Corneille's tragedies: the role of the unexpected
I. Title
842.4

ISBN 0–7083–1100–8

Typeset by Megaron, Cardiff, Wales
Printed by Billing and Sons, Worcester, England

Contents

Acknowledgements

I wish to thank the editors and publishers who have permitted me to use material from the following papers:

'*Horace*, première tragédie classique,' *Mélanges d'histoire litteraire (XVIe–XVIIe siècle) offerts à Raymond Lebègue par ses collègues, ses élèves et ses amis* (Nizet, 1959), pp. 195–200;
'*Médée*, almost a classical tragedy', *Romance Studies*, IV (1984), pp. 17–27;
'From *Pompée* to *Pertharite*', *Seventeenth-Century French Studies*, VII (1985), pp. 17–26
'Le sens de *Pertharite*', *Mélanges de littérature française offerts à René Pintard* (Strasbourg, 1975), pp. 175–84;
'Que devient l'héroïsme dans les tragédies "matrimoniales"?', *Pierre Corneille: actes du colloque tenu à Rouen du 2 au 6 octobre 1984*, ed. A. Niderst (PUF, 1985), pp. 255–31;
'Quand un héros soupire: the sad case of Sertorius', *Humanitas: Studies in French Literature presented to Henri Godin*, ed. R.L. Davis, J.H. Gillespie, R. McBride (Belfast, 1985), pp. 23–32;
'Othon, the unheroic hero', *Papers on French Seventeenth-Century Literature*, XI (1984), pp. 595–608.

Introduction

Safe as he may feel behind the Channel, a scholar from these shores who presumes to write on a great French playwright must know he will look a little foolish, a little childish, when he shows that he thinks the proper thing to write about is the way in which the plays were written, and how well they were written. Corneille, we are told today, was above all a great political thinker. It seems odd that the author of the finest tragedies before Racine, the inventor, virtually, of that tremendous genre, should have produced them not, as he said he had, to please the public, but as a sort of piecrust for blackbird pies to hide the products of his political meditations until it was three hundred years too late for them to be recognized as such, and relevant. I come with nothing to offer in elucidation of Corneille's thought. For me he is the poet of thousands of fine verses, the writer of scores of pages of closely reasoned argument, but not one, nor even a letter that we know of, on the state of the kingdom. He was a respectable scholar, but an expositor of Aristotle's *Poetics*, not of Plato's *Republic*. He had read a lot of history, which he used as a record of events that he need not try to reconcile with *vraisemblance*, since they had actually happened; not, like Grotius, as a repertory of precedents for a new jurisprudence.

I am willing to believe that he was aware of contemporary ideas and used them in his plays: not that he used his plays to embody them.[1] Of course he must have reflected, though perhaps he was too prudent to talk very much, on the perils of his times. And of course his tragedies contain captains and kings, counsellors, courtiers and conspirators; for he knew that tragedy concerned itself with the great ones of the earth, and Scaliger had laid it down that its themes were

> kings and princes, taken from cities, citadels and camps, . . . edicts of kings, deaths, despair, hangings, exiles, . . .[2]

His ideas on kingship or *raison d'Etat* do not seem to me very important or very essential to the understanding of his plays. More important to me is the fact that everyone agrees that three of these tragedies, and one tragicomedy, are admirable, while many critics have averted their eyes from the other seventeen, and many readers have excused themselves from the trouble of reading them. This is a pity, and something I should like to help to rectify; for they are, if not as emotionally stirring as the best, intellectually fascinating, and the contrast they form with the Tetralogy must hold some part of the secret of Corneille's great and rather melancholy career.

I hope no reader will open this book looking for a systematic and exhaustive study. Many of its interpretations and suggestions – they do not pretend to be 'explanations' – have appeared separately elsewhere;[3] and if in consequence it bears a slightly episodic appearance I shall not be sorry, for I am chary of seeming to propose any systematic theory of what, as we say, 'made him write' his plays.

I
Towards Tragedy

Years ago – before my time – it was usual to present the history of French tragedy as a march, with inevitable mistakes, towards a blazing beacon of a model, not very distant but there all the time. Landmarks there were in plenty behind them, which most were pretty determined to ignore, but none of course in front, which is what makes the achievement of Corneille so remarkable.

For he was the pioneer; and though he did not write the earliest of the new group of plays called tragedies that erupted in 1634, it was he who found the style and the spirit which all his coevals sooner or later followed, while their efforts had nothing to teach him.

It would be presumptuous to pretend to be able to reproduce the workings of the young playwright's imagination, but it is possible to see what guidance he could have found, what advantages he had, what impulsions could have helped him forward.

Like his fellows, he had had time to learn his craft in other genres. He made a remarkable success in Rouen, at the age of twenty-three, far from the theatre and movements of Paris, with a comedy unlike all that had appeared before. It made the fortune of the company which accepted his play and took it to Paris. He wrote a string of four comedies, broken by one odd experiment in 1631 or 1632, which brought a new type of action and subject matter to the old framework of comedy which had worked on Italian models – a type in part derived from the love-plots of pastoral, in part a (fairly) realistic picture of the social world the author knew and moved in. He learnt to use the machinery of drama as it then worked; he learnt to make his characters speak with some naturalness in verse dialogue; and he learnt to excel all his rivals in every resource of the French dramatic alexandrine.

He can with equal justice be considered as the creator of what we now call French 'classical tragedy'. His first tragedy, *Médée*, produced only a year after the 1634 breakthrough, had not yet found the secret. Nor had the works of his rivals in those years, a mere handful of commendable experiments, anything to teach him. He could – and no doubt did – learn from their mistakes, though he has left no sign of this, since his principle was never to criticize contemporaries in his theoretical discussions: the one exception was *Mariane* (1636) by

Tristan who died in 1654. Here he found the scenes of Herod's remorse after his wife's execution in Act V much too long, because the audience had nothing to wait for. He admits it was successful; but he adds (in 1660): 'Je ne conseillerais à personne de s'assurer sur cet exemple. Il ne se fait pas de miracles tous les jours . . . ' (B26)'

The tragedies of the old humanists, Jodelle, Garnier, Montchrestien, were justly neglected. He could but read the treatises the theorists kept quoting and the precedents of ancient drama – but there he was blocked because he did not read Greek (probably only the Latin translations of plays, usually printed with them) and had only the unhelpful example of Seneca's undramatic rhetoric to stir his imagination. He has left on record that he was unaware in 1629 that *les règles* existed. (*Les règles* were, simply, the three Unities of Time, Place and Action, a Renaissance invention applied and then forgotten in France, which his contemporary Mairet had lately reimported for use in Pastorals.) By 1634 he has found out what he thinks about them and is prepared to promise: 'Quelque jour je m'expliquerai davantage sur ces matières' (B177). By 1637 he is up to his eyes in the battle of pamphlets occasioned by his too successful and much combated play *Le Cid*, and in a spirited manifesto in the form of a dedication he announces a highly qualified and independent acceptance of 'ces grands maîtres des autres siècles: les règles des anciens':

> J'aime à suivre les règles; mais loin de me rendre leur esclave, je les élargis et resserre selon le besoin qu'en a mon sujet. Savoir les règles, et entendre le secret de les apprivoiser adroitement avec notre théâtre, ce sont deux sciences bien différentes; et peut-être que pour faire maintenant réussir une pièce, ce n'est pas assez d'avoir étudié dans les livres d'Aristotle et d'Horace. J'espère un jour traiter ces matières plus à fond, et montrer de quelle espèce est la vraisemblance . . . (B179)

The promised disquisitions did not appear till 1660, though he made certain remarks in reissuing *Le Cid* in 1648. Meanwhile it was quite true that he thought it not enough to have pored over the *Poetics* and Horace's *Ars Poetica*; he had to rely on painful trial and error.

Clitandre: tragicomedy within the rules

No sooner had the young poet made his name than he did as he was often to do in later years, and deserted the medium that had brought him success, for something else that might seem a greater novelty to the public.

The tragicomedy at that moment was the rallying-ground of opposition to the Unity of Time, a doctrine lately reintroduced by Mairet and taken up by such theoretical critics as Chapelain. Two forces which were to shape 'classical' tragedy were here opposed – the taste for 'regularity', the desire for *vraisemblance*, the desire to consult the ancient authorities on drama, and principally Aristotle's *Poetics* (misinterpreted); and against this the taste – which must have been that of a different public – for movement and variety on the stage.

'La poésie, et particulièrement celle qui est faite pour le théâtre, n'est faite que pour le plaisir et le divertissement', wrote a young writer François Ogier in a preface[2] manifesto of 1628 which Corneille seems clearly to have had in his memory; 'et ce plaisir ne peut procéder que de la variété des événements qui s'y représentent'. He objects particularly to the 'messengers' speeches' by which events were worked in, which the 24-hour rule prevented the playwright from exhibiting. 'De sorte que, presque à tous les actes, ces messieurs entretiennent la compagnie d'une longue déduction de fâcheuses intrigues qui font perdre patience à l'auditeur. Il est plus commode à une bonne hostellerie qu'il n'est convenable à une excellente tragédie d'y voir arriver incessamment des messagers'.[3]

Corneille, with the courage of the young, undertook to reconcile these two requirements – no tragicomedy had even tried before *Clitandre* to subject itself to the rules. What he thought he had to do was to squeeze into the stage action 'les choses merveilleuses qui arrivent *aux* personnages' yet to keep the rule: 'me tenant dans la contrainte de cette méthode, j'en *ai* pris la beauté sans tomber dans les inconvénients que les Grecs and les Latins, qui l'ont suivie, n'ont su d'ordinaire ou du moins n'ont osé éviter' (*Préface*). He failed of course; he notices that the play had proved hard to follow, 'vu que les narrations qui doivent donner le jour au reste y sont si courtes que le moindre défaut, ou d'attention du spectateur, ou de mémoire de l'acteur, laisse une obscurité perpétuelle en la suite . . . '. He packed *Clitandre* with violent action – two deaths on stage, an attempted rape and an eye put out with a brooch, an arrest – of a character who, as it happens, most passively languishes in gaol awaiting execution. Presumably Corneille taught himself a useful lesson – that speech is positively useful in expounding and commenting on the action, and indeed can be action itself; this happens, not so visibly in *Médée*, but in *Horace*, *Cinna* and *Polyeucte*; in three of these four of course he cannot show the most important events of the action.

Médée: almost a tragedy

The background of *Médée* is fairly well known,[4] but it may be helpful to recall certain points. First, the fact that just before 1630 the dramatic Unities had returned. Second, the fact that, as we have seen, interest and curiosity about the 'règle des vingt-quatre heures' met with understandable opposition from writers of the other popular dramatic genre, tragicomedy. Third, the strong probability that somebody realized that tragedy had been first written by the ancients, whose plays were the supposed precedent from which the Unities had been developed; and hence the assumption that it would be no trouble to square new tragedies with the 24-hours rule.

So it was, or so it seems, that Rotrou produced on the stage of the Hôtel de Bourgogne, in February 1634, the tragedy of *Hercule mourant*, adapted from *Hercules Oetaeus* by Seneca. Mairet's *Sophonisbe*, brought out on the other Paris theatre, that of the Marais, later the same year, revived a different but equally old tradition, that of tragedy based on ancient history – to which Rotrou and Corneille were to rally later on: Corneille never returned to ancient myth except under the pressure of a patron or impresario. But Corneille in his first tragedy, also for the Marais (March-April 1635), had quite possibly been invited or encouraged to put up a piece to copy and compete with Rotrou's, and that is what he did. Rotrou's subject had been the death of Hercules through a poisoned garment sent to him by his neglected wife, and his subsequent apotheosis: Corneille took another Senecan subject of conjugal jealousy and magic poison, that of Medea's vengeance on her husband (who had deserted her for the daughter of the King of Corinth) by killing his new bride with a poisoned robe, and by murdering his sons.

Not that these two young men – Corneille was twenty-seven at the time of *Hercule*, Rotrou not yet twenty-five – would have renewed tragedy if they had known only Seneca. Both were popular writers in the popular genres of the day: Rotrou, who that year terminated an eight-year contract with the Hôtel de Bourgogne, claimed authorship of thirty plays, of which we know eleven (six comedies and five tragicomedies);[5] Corneille had produced five successful comedies and one rather odd tragicomedy in five years, all for the rival troupe now at the Marais. (Mairet, who was then thirty, had a similar record, and moreover the credit of having brought back the Unities from Italy.) A curious point is that Corneille, always an experimenter, is here an imitator, and the imitator of a younger man. But Rotrou had more experience. And Corneille wrote the better play.

Rotrou's Hôtel de Bourgogne was old, and must have had a plentiful stock of scenery: it went to town on *Hercule mourant*.[6] 'Le théâtre doit estre superbe'; it showed a temple (where Hercule sacrificed), a 'chambre funèbre' (for his body), a prison (a barred window, through which a touching interview takes place), a mountain (practicable) and a lavishly decorated 'salle' (some of these curtained off until needed).

The Théâtre du Marais was no doubt poorer in scenery (the theatre had been new in 1634); it was also serving most of the young generation of playwrights observing Unity of Place of a sort, and so needing a simpler décor. Mairet's *Sophonisbe* requires only three settings: a 'room in the palace', a scene outside the city (used once, II. 1), easily indicated by drawing a set of front 'tabs', and a back room (IV. 2–3; V. 4–5, 7–8) created apparently by drawing back another set of 'tabs' upstage.

Corneille's set in *Médée* represents a public place, as in the two ancient plays on the same subject, by Euripides and Seneca. Corneille says so in his *Examen* of 1660, and apologizes for the fact; he held, like everyone else, that 'nous ne prenons pas la même liberté de tirer les rois et les princesses de leurs appartements' because their speeches are not for all to hear.[7] There is no other tragedy in which he does this. It requires a palace (presumably dominating the back of the stage) and a house, from which emerge respectively the King and Médée. Her house has a room ('cabinet' or 'grotte', where she is seen making a magic brew), and a 'balcon', which is surely the upper stage, from which she mounts the dragon chariot in the denouement. There is also a 'prison' for Egée[8] (they were in favour in the 1630s, though Corneille came to dislike them; see the *Examen*). Egée has no other lodging provided.

So *Médée* keeps the Unity of Place more neatly than *Hercule*. The Unities of Time and Action are guaranteed by Seneca, the source. As we have all been taught, the Unities should have produced an increase in simplicity (at least of a kind), internal intensity and external sobriety. But, paradoxically, what must have been a more prominent consideration for Rotrou – and therefore probably for Corneille too – was of an almost diametrically opposite nature: the possibility of spectacular effects. Stage machinery, already much used in Italy, was just coming to Paris; and both our plays employ a crane or some system of winches in the (no doubt very restricted) 'flies' which could lift, move, or lower scenery or actors. Rotrou's Hercule, deified in the fifth act, descends on a cloud and returns to heaven: Médée, not be outdone, has her team of dragons (both episodes appear in Seneca, so his influence is ambivalent).

> *Médée, en l'air dans un char tiré par deux dragons.*
> Epargne, cher époux, les efforts que tu perds,
> Vois les chemins de l'air qui me sont tous ouverts,
> C'est par là que je fuis. (1567 ff.)
> *Jason* O dieux! Ce char volant, disparu dans la nue,
> La dérobe à sa peine, aussi bien qu'à ma vue . . . [9]
> (1581 f.)

The wording would seem to contradict J. Golder's assertion that, since the Marais had no machinery, the chariot must have been sitting on the roof of a building, and then concealed by painted clouds hung like washing on a line (such as we know were used to hide the flies from the audience).[10] Yet – second paradox – the most spectacular element in both was not only not mechanical but invisible: the magically produced flames which devour the body of Rotrou's hero (*Hercule* III. 1–2; IV. 1–2, 4) and of two victims in Corneille, Créon and his daughter, Médée's rival (V. 2–4), both in protracted scenes exploiting their agonies to the full.

Seneca's well-known love of horror is usually confined to his *récits*, as such episodes are in Euripides, but not in *Hercules Oetaeus*: the dying hero raves on the stage, though it has to be understood (supposing the Roman tragedy was really performed) that the fire was miraculously invisible. Rotrou had only to copy.

Corneille on the other hand had to invent his scenes, rather than let Rotrou beat him (141 lines of lament, for Créon solus, then Créon and Créuse, then Créuse and Jason), out of a single line (880) in the account of Seneca'a messenger, who is more interested in the blaze in the palace. Corneille can at times be very fussy about minor questions of *vraisemblance* (the major ones worry him less – 'le sujet d'une belle tragédie doit n'être pas vraisemblable'):[11] he makes his messenger say, before the victims enter, 'La flamme disparaît, mais l'ardeur leur demeure' (1334/1314).[12]

The legendary Medea had possessed these magic powers (as Dejanira the wife of Hercules did not). Seneca had emphasized them, much more than Euripides, and Corneille used them with gusto. He takes over Seneca's scene of the brewing of the poison, though he edits it severely; and he adds two other, less effective, conjuring tricks of his own invention – when Médée lets Egée out of prison and sends him off, led by her confidant carrying a torch conferring invisibility (changed in later editions to the magic ring of so many pastorals, 1292 ff./1280 ff.), and later immobilizes the messenger with a tap of her wand to make him stay and tell his tale (1311 ff./1295 ff.).

There is in fact a youthful exuberance in this play (the fashionable word is 'baroque'). Corneille ends it with every character but the heroine dead, except utilities and soldiers (Racine was to do just the same in his first play, *La Thébaïde*); for Jason, who survived in other versions, stabs himself here.

But if three principal characters are allowed to die in full view, as the hero will do in *L'Illusion*, Médée's two children are not, though in the Seneca play they are. They do not appear in Corneille's cast (Paris theatres very rarely used children in this century), and perhaps we need seek no other reason: but after all Horace's *Ars Poetica* had explicitly forbidden these murders *coram populo* (185). The *Examen* of 1660 shows the poet excessively conscious, twenty-five years later, of the care with which he had treated points of *bienséance* and *vraisemblance*; with regard to the Argonaut Pollux whom he had brought in for dramatic convenience, and more particularly with regard to Egée. Euripides had given Aegeus a brief appearance, to assure Medea of a safe refuge in Athens after her revenge (Seneca drops him altogether), but once introduced Egée needs, says Corneille, a bigger and better-integrated part. A bigger part he certainly gets, though perhaps not perfectly integrated: he loves Créuse, is rejected, and tries to carry her off by force of arms. Corneille does not add that by freeing him Médée gives him more suitable grounds for gratitude – how could she promise, as she had in Euripides, to cure him of his childlessness?

Neither French dramatist was content to follow Seneca's plots as they stood. Rotrou's model, *Hercules Oetaeus*, reveals its author's lack of stage sense at its worst – he never shows Iole with the hero, nor with his jealous wife: the French adapter puts this right and even builds a new triangle situation introducing Arcas, who is loved by the captive girl and threatened by her captor.

The Latin *Medea* was better than *Hercules*; there was movement and it was expressed and furthered in scenes of violent confrontation. Medea, already planning vengeance, faces Creon and gains a day's grace before banishment; she reproaches Jason, and this time demands to take the children with her, but Jason loves them too much; so she now sees how to punish him as well as Creon and Creusa, proceeds with the two sets of murders, then defies Jason and flies off. But Seneca failed to bring the princess on to the stage: Corneille does this, giving her three scenes with Jason, whose role is enormously (six times) enlarged, one with Egée, and a long death-scene (V. 3–4).

Where Seneca strings his scenes together between choruses and monologues expressive of horror and frenzy, Corneille is conscious – more so than Rotrou – of the need for that causal nexus between successive incidents (*post hoc* et *propter hoc*) demanded by the *Poetics*;[13] and the endings of Acts I, II and III show that he is already creating suspense to carry the audience's curiosity over the intervals. The detailed story of the means and stages by which these hallmarks of the 'classical' system came into tragedy would be interesting, and it may be that enough evidence is at our disposal for someone to attempt it.

Seneca and his Renaissance disciples had not attempted much by way of character delineation – little beyond the motivation for the acts the plot required, and *exempla* of moral qualities. But the figure of Medea is, for its passionate intensity if not its profundity, one of the three great female figures of ancient drama, worthy to stand beside Clytemnestra and Phaedra. She is deeply impressive in Corneille's play, though she benefits perhaps from the ease with which we can interpret her consciousness of irresistible power as the unflinching will of later heroines like Cornélie or Cléopâtre (in *Rodogune*). When she answers her confidant in the much-quoted passage:

> Dans un si grand revers que vous reste-t-il?
>
> – Moi,
>
> Moi, dis-je, et c'est assez.
>
> – Quoi! vous seule, Madame?
>
> –Oui, tu vois en moi seule et le fer et la flamme,
> Et la terre, et la mer, et l'enfer et les cieux . . . (316/320 ff.)

She is scarcely exaggerating the real, material power that her magic confers on her. Nor can I see in her, as A. de Leyssac does, 'une héroïne du devoir',[14] even in the (decidedly special) sense given to that word by O. Nadal, whom he quotes: 'Dans ce théâtre, le devoir ne consiste pas en définitive à être juste, bon, honnête, mais à satisfaire la gloire . . . '[15] I find one use (stoical) of the verb *devoir*:

> L'âme doit se roidir plus elle est menacée; (305/309)

but her constant appeal is to her rights, to justice. She has indeed, as much as the Cléopâtre of *Rodogune*, 'le caractère brillant et élevé'[16] of the moral quality she represents – in her case an evil one: she is malignant, deceitful, thoroughly dangerous. If she appeals to pity, at rare moments, as an exile deprived of a refuge (788/776), it is partly a pose, partly perhaps a reminiscence, through Seneca (453), of the other Medea of Euripides, whose wrongs and whose helplessness were played up and her magic power played down, to make her an object of commiseration even more than of terror. Corneille knew them both, and confessed his preferences in the Latin verses he sent to Christian Huyghens with a copy of the play fourteen years later:[17] Euripides, he says, showed her *trementem*, Seneca *tremendam*, and his figure owed nothing to the first, but 'much, too much' to the second. We have seen that he did not totally ignore Euripides; but he was not capable, even had he wished, of blending a victim-figure of the latter with a raging maenad of Seneca as Racine was to do in *Phèdre*.

Jason is a lightweight beside her, though in his way even more unpleasant. He comes from Corneille's early comedies, one of those 'coureurs de dot' who has risen in the world to become an 'amoureux par maxime d'Etat' (28, first edition), as he describes himself with cynical vanity. He appears again, with the same rather black-comic style, in the earlier episode of his career which supplied the machine-play *La Conquête de la Toison d'Or* of 1660.

In fact the two Jasons remind us, as does Médée herself, that the most permanent element in Corneille's tragic canon is not idealized nobility but evil studied in its strength or weakness – the inhuman side of passion, or the ignoble side of what he termed *la politique*, the second motive force which is never absent by the side of love (and here in his first tragedy is far more important). Jason the unprincipled will be followed, with all sorts of nuances, by Maxime, Felix, Ptolomée and his court, Valens, Prusias, Garibalde . . . down to Othon's cronies and beyond.

So *Médée* strikes a balance between two wrongs, showing already the skill its author was to develop as advocate, or speech-writer, in duty bound to supply all his clients with the best available arguments. Balance – antithesis, dilemma – will always be a great resource of Corneille's art; in the 'great Tetralogy' it will be a dilemma between two goods, between which the scale of priority has to be determined with anxiety and pain by the hero. It is the answer that he gives – the willingness to give an answer – that defines heroism.

Euripides, far better than Seneca, had given a hint of this painful choice (not, here, between good and good); but Corneille's heroine's resolve does not begin to be a challenge to herself, a soul-struggle as H.C. Lancaster somewhat quaintly calls it, till his fifth act when, with Créon and Créuse already dead, she sees the cost to herself in striking at Jason through his love for their children. The anguish of decision comes a little earlier in the play to Euripides' heroine, when she sees her plan of action clear and has to put it in motion:

What makes me cry with pain
Is the next thing I have to do. I will kill my sons.
No one shall take my children from me. (791 ff.)

The Chorus expostulates: 'You must not do this' (813), and later:

Where will you find hardness of purpose?
How will you build resolution in hand or heart
To face horror without flinching?
When the moment comes, and you look at them . . .
Your heart will melt; you will know you cannot. (846 ff.)

Medea does waver again, but hardens her heart to bid farewell to her children (as they go with the poisoned robe to Creusa).

Now we must say goodbye. Oh, darling hand,
And darling mouth; your noble, childlike face and body!
Dear sons, my blessing on you both – but there, not here!
All blessing here your father has destroyed. How sweet
To hold you! And children's skin is soft, and their breath pure.
Go! Go away! I can't look at you any longer.
My pain is more than I can bear. I understand
The horror of what I am going to do; but anger,
The spring of all life's horror, masters my resolve.[18] (1070 ff.)

This human naturalness is foreign to Seneca; it is not his vein at all. Perhaps he sees the possibilities; but he falls into his usual bombast (with a vision of the Furies), he balances concepts, and chops logic, seeking his effects in epigrammatic paradox and antithesis.

Egone ut meorum liberum ac prolis meae
fundam cruorem? . . .
quod scelus miseri luent?
Scelus est Iason genitor et maius scelus
Medea mater: occidant, non sunt mei;

pereant, mei sunt . . .
Quid, anime, titubas? . . . (929–37)
Ira pietatem fugat
Iramque pietas. – Cede pietati, dolor. (944–45)

Corneille seems really to try, but to lack the stylistic resources. He also lacked the possibility of bringing children on the stage, for a last embrace; but he cannot imagine this kind of passion from the inside. His Médée, after the imitations of Seneca, describes her emotions to us, argues, and even analyses them. Sabine, Emilie or Pauline will do much the same, but they will convince us better.

Est-ce assez, ma vengeance, est-ce assez de deux morts?
Consulte avec loisir tes plus ardents transports . . .
Que n'a-t-elle [Créuse] déjà des enfants de Jason? . . .
Suppléons-y des miens . . .
Nature, je le puis sans violer ta loi:
Ils viennent de sa part et ne sont plus à moi.
Mais ils sont innocents? aussi l'était mon frère:
Ils sont trop criminels d'avoir Jason pour père . . .
Mais quoi! j'ai beau contre eux animer mon audace,
La pitié la combat et se met en sa place,
Puis, cédant tout à coup la place à ma fureur,
J'adore les projets qui me faisaient horreur:
De l'amour aussitôt je passe à la colère,
Des sentiments de femme aux tendresses de mère.
Cessez dorénavant, pensers irrésolus,
D'épargner des enfants que je ne verrai plus . . .
Mais ma pitié renaît et revient me braver;
Je n'exécute rien, et mon âme éperdue
Entre deux passions demeure suspendue.
N'en délibérons plus, mon bras en résoudra . . .
(1347 ff./1327 ff.)

Racine could feel and follow Euripides as Corneille never could; probably Corneille preferred other dramatic effects which suited him better. Here he is working in the spirit of the *imitatio* recommended by the rhetorical tradition. The exercise has been profitable, if only as an exercise in acquiring the tragic register of style.

Though he had learned much, Corneille would still need a second invigorating plunge into tragicomedy, and long and painful reflection provoked by the *Querelle du Cid*, before he could create 'classical' tragedy with *Horace*. He was not Rodrigue, and needed a few *coups d'essai*. *Médée* was one.

L'Illusion comique: that final 'tragedy'

L'Illusion comique, written probably soon before *Le Cid*, contains a fragment that Corneille calls a tragedy (he calls it so in a dedication of 1639), but we must not look to *L'Illusion comique* to reveal any serious thinking by the poet about the genre. The scenes 2–4 of Act V constitute a play-within-the-play-within-the-play which is intended (by the poet) to trick one of the characters, as well as the audience, into taking it as a 'real' event, of a piece with the 'real' action of Act IV 1–9, whereas what has been seen is a tragedy, or rather a snatch of a tragedy, being performed in a professional theatre: a *mage* has devised the world's earliest video system, operated for him by subject spirits (like Prospero's), by means of which he is obligingly enlightening an anxious father about the doings of a son he has disinherited. After a gap in the time-sequence, the son, last seen escaping from prison, is (to all appearances) a highly-placed courtier conducting a love-intrigue with his prince's wife, and getting stabbed for his sins. Corneille has not given much thought to his 'tragic' action – it is only an episode, and its naïvety of treatment and sententious moralizing remind us of a work of A. Hardy. The scene might be a pastiche of Hardy – and why not, since his was still the best-known type of tragedy? The only difference is that the language is far less archaic: it has to be, otherwise the contrast with Corneille's dialogue elsewhere in the play would give away the trick at once. The forsaken wife (acted by the hero's mistress) catches her husband before his assignation in a garden and reproaches him; he attempts to excuse his lapse, then is suddenly converted, and attempts in his turn to dissuade his mistress when she arrives.

Such moralizing over marital fidelity will never appear in Corneille's real tragedies; nor will the conclusion, or either of the pair of alternative conclusions given in successive editions, in the first of which, after the stabbing (on stage) of the two lovers by the prince's men, the wife receives an invitation from the prince, and is led off with no indication whether she will accept or no; in the amended version (1639) she either swoons or dies. The playwright's only interest is to delude the spectators (on stage and in the house) into taking the violent conclusion as the 'real' death of the character whose adventures they have been following, and so being delighted and surprised when the next scene shows him with his fellow-actors peacefully counting up the night's takings. We have only to say that Corneille showed his opinion of contemporary tragedy – in the provinces – by putting into his pastiche features that he never used in any of his plays, whether called tragedies or not. His thoughts were not on the nature of tragedy, but rather on dramatic illusion. He needed that death on the stage to work his trick, and the rules of the genre concerned him not at all.

II
The Tetralogy

The five years after *L'Illusion* are a time of great originality, great achievement; they also include the only literary quarrel Corneille ever entered, and a remarkable change of direction, from the genre called tragicomedy back to tragedy, which Corneille transformed.

So many critical studies confine themselves to the four great plays of the period (the 'Tetralogy', the tragicomedy *Le Cid* and the tragedies, *Horace*, *Cinna* and *Polyeucte*) that I hope I shall be excused – especially as I have written a small book on *Horace*[1] – for passing lightly over issues that have become rather threadbare. I shall limit myself to saying why I admire these tremendous plays, to pointing to some of the discoveries their author made and some of the difficulties he encountered in them, and to making some other points where I think I may have something new to say.

Le Cid: heroism with a Spanish swagger

Corneille only entered the world of 'Cornelian' heroism in the Tetralogy, and only rarely re-entered it after. He came across *Las Mocedades del Cid*, an early *comedia* of Guillén de Castro[2] published in 1618. It sets out to be the epic story of the rise to fame of a warrior-hero of folklore, but it contains a well-developed love story – of a couple united and divided by the cult of honour. There was of course much for Corneille to leave out in this sprawling drama innocent of any of the Unities: the hero moves about here and there to conquer the King's enemies; there are hints of dissentions in the royal family, because they will become important in the Second Part (*Las hazanas del Cid*) already planned. But the heart-searchings of the Infanta, an undeclared rival of Ximena Gomez, Corneille for some reason did not suppress. Unlike Shakespeare, Castro never attempts to show on his stage any of the feats of arms that abound in his story. Corneille follows him, and abandons perforce that ambition he had proclaimed in his earlier tragicomedy – to stage all the striking actions in full view; there will be no physical action in any play of his from now on, except for the one isolated 'soufflet' in the *Cid*, and, if you will, Camille's absurd dash for the exit in order to be murdered in the wings by Horace.

In the situation of the estranged lovers shown in Castro's play (prominently shown, for the quarrel of their parents and the unforgivable *bufetada* occur very early, and the announcement of their imminent marriage provides the denouement) Corneille found all the elements of balance, antithesis and paradox which were to give *Le Cid* its pathos and its tension. He had only to disentangle them, bring them into a pattern and tighten their connections. Thus, Castro had made it clear (by multiple asides – a device Corneille disliked)[3] that Ximena loves Rodrigo de Bivar, and reasonably clear that he loves her: but Corneille uses his opening scene to show that this day is, by a disastrous coincidence, to see the formal *demande en mariage* – Chimène is in an ecstasy of impatience and anxiety. The story unfolds much as Corneille makes it, if more slowly, the quarrel between two boastful grandees (in which the King himself is defied), the blow, the charge to the son, his agonized deliberation where the rhymes make the refrain:

> ¿ . . . que fuese
> mi padre el ofendido, ¡ estraña pena!
> y el ofensor el padre de Ximena? (523 ff.)

> (That my father should be the one offended – unwonted pain! – if the offender the father of Ximena.)

But the Spanish Rodrigo does not debate his dilemma with himself, though the issues are clear, nor does he even contemplate seeking death; the decision to defend his honour is a sudden gut-reaction. In the same way Ximena's resolve to claim justice, and even her refusal to be content with a refusal, are spontaneous decisions. But it is the meeting of the lovers (III. 4), the scene that scandalized French critical opinion but which Corneille refused to alter, that exhibits the principles of symmetry and antithesis in their fullest degree.

> Por mi honor, aunque muger,
> he de hazer
> contra ti quanto pudiere . . .
> deseando no poder.
> . . . (1196 ff.)
> Disculpara mi decoro
> con quien piensa que te adoro,
> el saber que te persigo. (1174 ff.)

> (For my honour, albeit a woman, I have to do all I can against you – yet desiring to be able to do nothing. – My good name will

be cleared, if anyone considers that I adore you, by the knowledge that I am seeking your punishment.)

But only Corneille makes her say she wants the world to know that her persecution is play-acting, and she will gain glory from that:

> Et je veux que la voix de la plus noire envie
> Elève au Ciel ma gloire et plaigne mes ennuis
> Sachant que je t'adore et que je te poursuis. (980/970ff.[4])

She admits that she cannot disapprove his action:

> yo confieso, aunque la sienta,
> que en dar vengança a tu afrenta
> como Cavallero hiziste. (1156 ff.)

(I confess that, much as it grieves me, in avenging the insult given to you, you acted like a [good] knight.)

And only Corneille makes her say she is doing as he does because he taught her to – she is doing it to be worthy of him (as *he* wanted to be worthy of her):

> Tu n'as fait le devoir que d'un homme de bien;
> Mais aussi, le faisant, tu m'as appris le mien; (921 ff./911 ff.)

In this way the two extremes balance and support each other like the columns of a Gothic arch – how could either stand, deprived of the other? Otherwise, we might judge Chimène as a woman unduly afraid of public opinion, or as a schoolgirl carried away by a stubborn and silly idealism: but Rodrigo had sacrificed her to his honour, as she reminds us, and she thinks he was right, 'adores' him, and seeks to emulate him – what if it is at his expense? He understands her.

In this splendid scene, Corneille has found the way to construct a strong clash of motives in the form – as so often later – of a debate; this time on the absurd motion that Chimène should kill Rodrigue there and then with his own sword; she, snatching at all the plausible arguments she can find, he gently refuting them (but does he really want to die in this way, or is he pressing her for the sake of extorting a disavowal of her resolve, as O. Nadal has persuasively suggested – but with too brutal an insistance on the ideas of mental cruelty and moral blackmail?).[5] The impassioned but logically reasoned speeches are full, not of moralizing, but of rhetorical questions and strong lines that are repeated and thrown back, all the more powerful for being echoes:

R. Car enfin n'attends pas de mon affection
Un lâche repentir d'une bonne action . . . (882/871 ff.)
CH. Car enfin n'attends pas de mon affection
De lâches sentiments pour ta punition: (937/927 ff.)
CH. De quoi qu'en ta faveur notre amour m'entretienne,
Ma générosité doit répondre à la tienne . . . (939/929 ff.)
R. De quoi qu'en ma faveur notre amour t'entretienne,
Ta générosité doit répondre à la mienne; (955/945 ff.)

Rodrigo, and Rodrigue, have solved their dilemma, each of them, in the first Act; thereafter they only have to win their fights – against the Count, the Moors, and the bereaved daughter's champion. Being by definition budding heroes, they find no difficulty there. But the lead, in Corneille if not so much in Castro, passes to Rodrigue's partner Chimène, and her struggle is far from over then – she feels compelled to repeat her demand for his punishment on every occasion, and reject every hope of accommodation; she dominates the play after their interview (though the Moors intervene to take up time and attention), or shares it only with her undeclared rival, 'l'Infante', so that this half could well be entitled *la Gloire de Chimène*. The number of her visits to the King to seek justice (four in Castro, reduced to three in *Le Cid*) worried Corneille (see his *Examen*) and tried the patience of Castro's King:

Tiene del Conde Loçano
la arogancia y la impaciencia. (1935 ff.)

(She takes her arrogance and impatience from Count Loçano [her father, but the name means Overbearing].)

But she may be excused because she has been put off so long – over two years. Corneille is able – and obliged – to make his choice among these incidents. He will suppress the bloody handkerchief she waves on her first appearance (889, stage direction); the retinue of servants in deepest mourning (1712, stage direction); the tale she tells (1973 – repeated from a popular *romance* and clearly false, cf. 1999 ff.) of Rodrigo's outrageous behaviour before her window, killing her doves. Her demand that the King authorize the offer she says she had already proclaimed of her hand or half her fortune to the man who brings her Rodrigo's head (2071) is transformed into a request for a champion, which is reluctantly granted with the proviso that she must wed the winner of the combat (*Cid* 1467/1457). Corneille shows here the strain he feels in preserving the 24-hour rule: 'Soyez prêt à demain', says the King, but Don Diègue, Rodrigue's father, protests:

> Non, Sire, il ne faut pas différer davantage:
> On est toujours trop prêt quand on a du courage.
> *Le Roi* Sortir d'une bataille et combattre à l'instant!
> *D.* Rodrigue a pris haleine en vous la racontant.
> *Le Roi* Du moins, une heure ou deux je veux qu'il se délasse.
> (1454 ff./1444 ff.)

What strips Chimène/Ximena of her pretence is the emotion she betrays at the false news of her lover's death – the effect is repeated twice by Castro, the trick being played for the second time by Rodrigo, a jest more acceptable from the playwright than from the hero, who might, one thinks, have considered his old father's feelings: the son has just defeated the champion of Aragon, the monstrous giant Don Martin, and has word sent that a knight is bringing Rodrigo's head to claim the lady's hand. The head is of course the one worn by Rodrigo, who nonchalantly adds that he has brought Martin's too, stuck on a lance (1975). Corneille replaces this unwanted comedy by a simple *quiproquo* or scene of cross purposes (see p. 22) – Chimène's false assumption has been prepared for by a second interview of the lovers (V. 1) in which Rodrigue once again insists on dying, this time by letting Sanche, the champion, kill him. After long debate he extorts the appeal from Chimène:

> Sors vainqueur d'un combat dont Chimène est le prix.
> Adieu! ce mot lâché me fait rougir de honte. (1566 ff./1534 ff.)

(This is the second of the *glissades* or *faux pas* – Corneille's own expressions – in which he allows her to succumb momentarily to the force of her passion.)

When therefore Sanche presents himself with a naked sword (having been disarmed and told to present it as a token of defeat) she has good cause for thinking Rodrigue is dead; and in a great outburst of passion, after cursing the unhappy Sanche with as much unreasoning ingratitude as Hermione with Oreste, she sweeps (so I believe) through all the barriers and stage conventions separating her *chambre* from the court-room, to lay bare her heart before the King. He and his counsellors knew of her love, admired her and had also smiled at her previous lies; but for a reconciliation, a public recantation is needed.

A happy ending, indeed a triumphant ending, was necessary for the heroic story of the Spanish *comedia*; and French tragicomedy was in no way opposed to the comic machinery that produces it, nor to the touches of comedy in the kindly trickery of the paternal King. I would not be 'reductionist' and deny P.H. Nurse[6] the liberty to consider the interpretation of this ending open. Corneille has written into Chimène's part (but only in 1682) some words of protest in the hope of placating the prophets of *bienséance* (1805 ff.); but it is difficult not to be affected by the buoyant optimism of the last words of the play, which Corneille never altered:

> *Rod.* ... Quoi qu'absent de ses yeux il me faille endurer,
> Sire, ce m'est trop d'heur de pouvoir espérer.
>
> *Le Roi* Espère en ton courage, espère en ma promesse,
> Et, possédant déjà le cœur de ta maîtresse,
> Pour vaincre un point d'honneur qui combat contre toi
> Laisse faire le temps, ta vaillance et ton Roi.
>
> (1861/1835 ff.)

And how could Corneille honestly pretend that he expected his public to understand the marriage as being doubtful? What sort of a denouement would that make?

Horace: the legacy of tragicomedy

After giving a tremendous boost to tragicomedy with *Le Cid*, Corneille did as we saw him do after *Clitandre* and *Médée*, turning away from successful experiments to make new ones. He went back to tragedy, which he had deserted after *Médée*, and began a long series of these works, beginning with those three which, because of their tone and outlook, we always link with *Le Cid* as the great Tetralogy. So many critics, dazzled by the brilliance of the Tetralogy, insist on treating it as if this were all that deserved to be looked at in the dramatist's immense output, or even – more modestly – as if these plays contained all elements necessary to understand the rest.

Horace did not mean a complete turning away from tragicomedy, it resembles *Le Cid* far more than it does *Médée* or any other of the recent tragedies; which is important because all future tragedies, his or, we may safely say, those of others, resemble *Horace* more than they do those earlier ones. It is worthwhile to consider in what respects *Horace* can be called tragicomic.

In the first place it is a love-story (*Cinna* and *Polyeucte* will contain love-stories too), as *Hercule mourant* and its contemporaries were not – the latter mostly show married characters suffering from jealousy (Rotrou's tragedy did, it is true, bring in a sub-plot with two young lovers, both threatened by Hercule.) But Horace boldly puts a couple of *jeunes premiers* in the centre – as they had also been in tragicomedy and earlier pastoral and as they were in *Le Cid*; they are Curiace and Camille, and it is curious to reflect that as it happened this is the pair that he found in his historical sources, whereas in working up a symmetrical situation, as he commonly did, it was Sabine that he had to invent, Horace's Alban wife.

It is not always noticed how different are these two symmetrical couples, chosen to illustrate in contrasting ways the pull between love and country. One is a settled couple married for two and a half years – Sabine could well have had children: if she has not, perhaps her husband has had too few leaves from active service, or more likely Corneille refused to encumber himself with any further complications. The two lovers are desperate; they have been separated by the war for two years, and now that they meet they hope and expect, under the truce, to marry the next day (114, 169 ff.). Do we always remember this to excuse, if not altogether the curses Camille utters against Rome, at least the lack of 'allégresse' Curiace shows in following the lead of Horace on the path of duty? This is no incidental detail buried in the action; Corneille introduces a bright gleam of hope with the oracle that has cheered Camille in Act I, and he closes the play – in both versions, though he shortens the definitive one – with a sorrowing reference to their broken hope. It was indeed Corneille who brought the love interest into tragedy, for all the distaste he was to express when a new infusion of tragicomedy took place into the (then rather sluggish) stream of tragedy. It was due largely to the success of what were called the 'tragédies galantes' of Corneille's younger brother Thomas, in the fifties; but it certainly brought in the dregs.

Other tragicomic features concern dramaturgy, the handling of the plot for the stage. Tragicomedy had been full of that favourite device of playwrights at a loss for credible means to make their characters do what the plot requires – *quiproquo* as they called it, the scene of cross-purposes, where characters, not even meaning to, mislead each other by speaking or acting in ways that are misinterpreted. In *Horace* the deceptive oracle is a device that had indeed been much used in the tragedies before; not so the scene where Camille flies to the false conclusion that her lover has deserted his post (243 ff.) and the false news of the duel brought in all innocence by the confidant (III. 6). Corneille will not allow these manufactured accidents to affect the outcome of the play; he liked his champions to know what they were doing and face each other *à visage découvert* (cf. p. 64); but they enable him to reveal a new and valuable facet in a character which but for the accident we should not have seen – Camille's scale of values with private affection well above all sense of patriotic duty, and that of *le vieil Horace*: *qu'il mourût*, that his son should have died rather than quit the field.

Horace recalls the tragicomedies in the third place by the linearity of its unfolding of the story. The 24-hour rule was forcing the playwright to reserve his five acts for the ending of his tragedy, with recalls to explain the rest; but like *Le Cid* (and unlike plays to follow) *Horace* begins as nearly as possible at the beginning – not with the marriage of Horace and the betrothal of Curiace that set up his two contrasting pairs of characters, it is true; but before the truce which comes before the duel, which is not even in prospect.

We see the same tendency in, for instance, Mairet. He had chosen in 1634 to put back the opening of his *Sophonisbe* a little before that of his immediate model *Sophonisbe* by Montchrestien, to a point when the battle of Syphax with the Romans is not even determined, and gains thereby three new uncertainties producing suspense – can the heroine explain away an intercepted letter? Will Syphax fight? Will he lose? Corneille even splits the choice of the combatants into two episodes, the duel into two narrations. Camille, crying out against the ordeals fate has inflicted on her, recounts quite faithfully the péripéties of the day's happenings:

En vit-on jamais un [un sort] dont les rudes traverses
Prissent en moins de rien tant de faces diverses,
Qui fût doux tant de fois, et tant de fois cruel,
Et portât tant de coups avant le coup mortel?
Vit-on jamais une âme en un jour plus atteinte
De joie et de douleur, d'espérance et de crainte,
Asservie en esclave à plus d'événements,
Et le piteux jouet de plus de changements?
Un oracle m'assure, un songe me travaille,
La paix calme l'effroi que me fait la bataille,
Mon hymen se prépare, et presque en un moment

Pour combattre mon frère on choisit mon amant;
Ce choix me désespère, et tous le désavouent,
La partie est rompue, et les Dieux la renouent;
Rome semble vaincue, et seul des trois Albains,
Curiace en mon sang n'a point trempé ses mains. (1203 ff.)

But the important revolution brought about by the tragicomedy – that in which Lanson, and many others since, have seen the nature of the new tragedy – is the fact that the interesting characters are not primarily those who suffer, but those who have to do something. Drama is conflict, we say; Corneille spoke of a threat, a 'péril' which formed the nub of the action of tragedy and gave it unity (V. p. 119). For Horace, Auguste or Polyeucte it is a challenge or an ordeal – which they intend if possible to surmount. This is new in tragedy: in Mairet's *Sophonisbe* on the contrary, Massinisse yields (to his love) and fights to save it, but hopelessly, and Sophonisbe is never seen to take a critical decision except to drink poison; in *Mariane* (Tristan, 1636) Hérode makes a decision, but has a whole act to repent it; Médée would have been more touching in her self-torture if everything had not been too easy for her as a magician. Whereas Horace, like Rodrigue, and Camille no less than Chimène, choose for themselves a difficult path and stick to it. Curiace owes his moral salvation to this – he chooses duty, and is swept away by the action. This is less easily seen in the roles of the women, who are not permitted the outlet of (martial) action – Sabine and Camille seem to have inherited the victim roles of old-style tragedy – supplications and laments. But in fact they do not supplicate or lament, and Corneille does not wish them to set this tone: they do not weep, they contrive to 'commander à *leurs* pleurs', as they weigh their emotions against one another; nor do they beseech, they argue their pleas with all the resources of logic, and even of fallacies. True, they lack the outlet of action, being women – until Camille joins the gentlemen and finds herself the solution of death, for which Sabine, maturer and more self-controlled, calls out in vain.

The motives the men obey would be easier for us to understand if we had read less about 'l'Éthique de la Gloire' in P. Benichou, O. Nadal and their school. The desire for fame is as old as Achilles in the *Iliad*. Horace seems to me an honest man of strong principles, which he proclaims once with rather bombastic rhetoric (but it is to encourage his friend, as L. Herland[7] has explained, and Corneille has just come from writing a tragicomedy based on a Spanish source) though he normally explains little and is afraid to debate with his wife (674); he expects and will be glad to have the approval and respect of his fellows after his unprecedented ordeal. He loses much sympathy today by his treatment of his wife: he seems to say that he is glad of the chance to bring pain to his loved ones, because it will bring him glory. What he says (431–52) is that few would be capable of wanting such a glory, but since it is a duty, and so painful, it is best to take it as a kind of compliment from 'le sort' to have thought Curiace and himself (he puts them together) capable of carrying it off.

I have said the women have no outlet but death, which is what Camille achieves. Poor Sabine has every reason to wish for it, with her husband and brother about to try to kill each other, and her seemingly mad proposal

> Qu'un de vous deux me tue et que l'autre me venge: (631)

– seems too fantastic to be taken seriously. But it is a serious challenge – not very *vraisemblable* perhaps, but brilliantly apt – an attempt to prove the falsity of their aspiration to *gloire* by doing what is difficult because so horrible. A touch more horror, she suggests, will make everything reasonable and fine. She makes an offer she does not expect to have to carry out, as a poker player bluffs – falsely over-calling his hand in the hope his opponent will shrink from matching his stake – and almost succeeds (663 ff.) in shaming the men out of their heroics. The same call for death, twice repeated with less irony, loses some of its force and pathos; nobody takes much notice and nothing is done to relieve her hopeless situation, except that the king and her father-in-law adjure her to do her duty and keep quiet (1635 ff., 1767 ff.). She is only a secondary character after all.

There was no irony in the grief she expressed for her country, Alba, doomed probably to defeat and subjugation. But one almost feels there is irony – probably unseen and unwilled by Corneille – in her protestation that any other act of aggression by Rome would have had her enthusiastic support:

> Bien loin de m'opposer à cette noble ardeur
> Qui suit l'arrêt des Dieux et court à ta grandeur,
> Je voudrais déjà voir tes troupes couronnées
> D'un pas victorieux franchir les Pyrénées. (45–48)

Corneille's quietly searching analysis of the immorality of wars of conquest has led him, by implication, to insinuate a denunciation of all war of which he was doubtless unaware, and which would probably have shocked him as much as anybody if he had realized it. But, ironically, it is to Roman imperialism, in which lay the origins of his crime, that Horace is sacrificed. Yet Corneille's determination to display all sides of this situation has turned this study of wartime patriotism into what can be read – by our eyes at least – into a protest against war.

Sabine and her brother were born to see two sides of a question. Camille and Horace are single-minded. In Corneille's repertory of conceivable responses to the clash of loyalties she champions the exclusive claims of personal affection, and pays for it. Corneille shows no acceptable solution: this is a tragedy – and that is why I hold him to be such a great dramatist. But Horace deserves some pity for the way he comes unsuspecting, after the excitement and horror of his contest, under her deliberate provocation (IV. 5). What he is feeling at this moment we cannot know: Herland thinks he is 'fou de douleur' and repressing unbearable grief and remorse: but the rule of *liaison des scènes* which he is now obeying gave Corneille no room for a monologue (or dialogue with Procule) like that of Camille (IV. 4).

Corneille has admitted in his *Examen* that this encounter brings his hero into a 'second péril' not necessarily related to the first, in fact a breach of the Unity of Action (cf. p.65). But not only did Livy's well-known history force him to break it – this story with its affronts to our sense of normality must have given Corneille intense satisfaction, not only by the 'unnatural' fight of the brothers-in-law, who indignantly refuse to be let off their duty (797 ff., drawn from Dionysius Halicarnassensis), but by the murder which

Vient de la même épée et part du même bras (1741)

(and is due to the same mentality) as brought victory to Rome.

The play does present a broken-backed appearance. Corneille has trouble with all the first three plays of the Tetralogy, which all shift the centre of interest in the middle of the action (from Rodrigue to Chimène, from Horace the victor to the murderer, from Cinna to Auguste). His history forced him to do this in *Horace*: but we see many signs of his desire, having built up a complex situation combining many factors and involving many characters, to exhibit every facet possible. It happens again in *Pertharite*.

The story-line also forced Corneille to end his play with a trial-scene, dropping the tension and showing no conflict but the clash of arguments developed in long speeches. There is indeed a certain painful interest in watching the behaviour of Horace. He is clearly far from the exultant mood of the beginning of Act IV, and knows his dearly-bought *gloire* has been lost; but he refuses to admit that he has done any wrong. Rather sullenly he invites the King to take his life, adding that it is worth little to him now. Not a soul judges that he has done rightly; not even his father (see 1416 ff.), though as his advocate he stoutly defends him. The King does not acquit him, he pardons him – for the same reason as Rodrigue was pardoned: that the state could not do without him.

It is a decidedly unhappy ending; perhaps Corneille still thought this necessary for a tragedy. But the fates of the three characters are not equally unhappy. One is pathetic, perhaps even heroic (though not quite in the sense we have defined for Corneille); one is pitiable and unresolved (Sabine's); the third is best seen as that of the man who has amputated his emotional self in a voluntary self-mutilation in order to do his duty.[8]

Cinna: tragedy with a happy ending

The Tetralogy is not a tetralogy in the same sense as the *Oresteia* is a trilogy. No character reappears, and settings differ, and the only family likeness to be traced in the heroes is the ability to make a hard and painful choice: the greater good to which they sacrifice rises successively from family (or personal) honour to *patrie*, to State, to God (and Corneille pointed this out in his dedication of *Polyeucte* to Anne of Austria). Horace can, though with some difficulty, be seen as a more developed Rodrigue; but Auguste breaks the chain – he has a criminal past and a troubled conscience, and needs inspiration from outside himself to find hisway of salvation, as he does at the very end of the play, and Auguste is balanced by two adversaries who are forced to recognize unheroically – though with some *générosité* – that the resolutions that had borne them along were falsely conceived.

Corneille in fact has been diligent in applying new touches to the rather bald story he found in Seneca or Montaigne – it tells simply that Augustus was once informed of a plot to kill him, passed a sleepless night contemplating the endless succession of plots he had to suppress, and accepted his wife Livia's advice to try the effect of clemency. He spent two hours in thoroughly humiliating the conspirator Cinna with his knowledge of the details of the plot and his contempt for the young man's unworthiness to aspire to the empire, and finally surprised him with the offer of pardon and even advancement, so that neither Cinna nor any other ever conspired against him again.

Retouching, in Corneille's mind, must have involved not only filling out the story, but redressing the balance between the parties, making one more worthy of the other and giving to each more dramatic and appealing antecedents (that antithetical mind could not accept a crude and simple contrast). No trouble in digging up the horrors of the proscriptions in which Augustus – as Octavius – had participated; but for the conspirator, whom he turned into a couple of conspirators, he seems to have had recourse to an expedient used once already in *Horace*, and often used later – he has invented a character to add to those provided by history and let this character give rise to a plot or sub-plot which seems to threaten the proportions of the whole structure. As we know this sub-plot is original, though a researcher may come across it some day in some forgotten romanesque source. Sabine, the invented character in *Horace*, opens that tragedy with her private dilemma (but does not turn it into an episode); Sévère bids fair to balance the interest in *Polyeucte*; as years later Dircé will fill the whole first act of *Oedipe* and almost make us forget the problem of the killer of Laïus and the guilt of his successor.

So, here in *Cinna*, we find as mainspring of the plot (against the life of Auguste) a young woman, Emilie, daughter of a victim of the proscriptions. (Young she must be, to enable her *beaux yeux* to inspire plots like so many romanesque schemers of Corneille's day; we must allow him to tamper with chronology, for it is unfitting to recall what D.A. Watts[9] has worked out, that she lost her father full forty-seven years before.) Emilie won great admiration from G. de Balzac and others, but wins a good deal less from the modern reader by her fixed fanatical desire for revenge, cherished over a lifetime. It is not very easy to believe that a child, adopted from infancy into the imperial family, and isolated from all other influences and examples, could have conceived or held to such a resolve, even to accepting kindnesses and gifts, and using the gifts to suborn potential rebels (79 ff.). She has attracted the love of Cinna, himself attached by birth to the defeated cause of Pompey; Cinna has sworn to avenge her by assassinating Auguste – not seeing too clearly that love was his motive rather than patriotism or any well-pondered political faith. Misguided is the description that fits them both best; it is hard to see why that good critic L. Herland should have been so thrilled by what he calls the purity and youthful passion of the two.[10]

We are plunged into this situation in Act I, which takes place in Emilie's *apartement* (presumably within Auguste's palace); it opens by showing the painful conflict in her heart between fear for Cinna's safety (for she loves him) and her relentless quest of vengeance. Cinna then recounts (I. 3) a secret meeting of the conspirators he has recruited, and a rousing speech he has made them about the crimes they are to punish. This may of course have been how seventeenth-century conspirators conducted their deliberations; if so it may account for their invariable failures. Then – *coup de théâtre* – a summons comes from the emperor for Cinna and his comrade Maxime, and it seems obvious that the plot has been discovered.

The second act is a bewildering contrast: we do not know where we are. The Auguste who appears is not the Auguste we had heard of, but a dignified, kindly man, affable, weary, disabused, but willing to listen and be convinced. The discussion he initiates is the debate as to whether he should return to private life – a debate which Dio Cassius recounts[11] as having taken place soon after the victory of Actium, long before, with Maecenas and Agrippa (both since dead). The Cinna who is obliged to give his opinion is very different from the fiery republican and would-be tyrannicide we had met – with great aplomb, eloquence and appearance of reason he argues that Auguste must not withdraw, for abdication would be construed as a condemnation of Caesar and all who had acquired power since, including Auguste himself. The argument is a dramatic surprise – probably no spectator or reader can guess the motive of these remarkable logical acrobatics, until the next scene furnishes the reason: it was to prevent Auguste from leaving power and so making the assassination unnecessary. It must have been insincere, for not even in later speech does Cinna disavow his hatred of 'tyranny' – but then, he gives plenty of reason, as we shall see, for doubting whether his beliefs have any strength or substance at all. Maxime has been more honest, and argued that Auguste would show generosity in restoring liberty to Rome, but he is overcome; the emperor rewards his two trusted counsellors by gifts of high offices, and to Cinna (additional irony) he gives the hand of Emilie.

When he decided to fill out his historically-founded tale with an invented action, Corneille presumably found considerable difficulty in fitting all the details into place. He speaks himself of *défauts* which had escaped notice (*Examen*). Certainly a number of them crop up as inconsistencies or unprepared surprises, which L. Herland has picked up in his recent (posthumous) study[12] – we are not warned of

Maxime's love for Emilie until his jealousy is aroused and becomes important; we are told only in line 1574 that the plot had been running over four years; Cinna speaks without any previous mention to Maxime of the 'vielle amitié' (855) that makes it hard for him to act against Auguste – as indeed it might and should have much earlier, before he had committed himself; only the Dramatis Personae tells us, before Emilie's last confrontation with Auguste (1599) that Toranius had been his guardian as well as her father (but would the fact seem as important to her as it was to him [1140]?).

The consultation of Auguste has wrecked the conspiracy without his knowledge; for he has left Cinna with an acute moral problem which will disarm him, and Maxime's conversation with Cinna gives Maxime a motive for the betrayal. To feel it impossible to accept Auguste's presents while still harbouring designs on his life shows a moral sensitivity that does him credit; but we are bound to feel that the situation is his own fault. Plenty of critics[13] have explained to us that the seventeenth century could understand but not fully feel emotions of patriotism and devotion to liberty, which they had met only in Latin exercises at school: the nobleman found his natural place and natural ties and duties, not in the patch of territory called his country, nor in any commonwealth, but under his king or feudal suzerain to whom he owed loyalty and from whom he expected protection and support. Cinna discovers the truth of this suddenly:

> Les douceurs de l'amour, celles de la vengeance,
> La gloire d'affranchir le lieu de ma naissance,
> N'ont point assez d'appas pour flatter ma raison,
> S'il les faut acquérir par une trahison,
> S'il faut percer le flanc d'un prince magnanime
> Qui du peu que je suis fait une telle estime,
> Qui me comble d'honneurs, qui m'accable de biens, (878 ff.)

and we are prompted to ask if he cared very much for avenging Toranius, or for the liberty of Rome, or anything but Emilie (and her memory is in eclipse now). The new remorse has swept away all other thoughts:

> Dure, dure à jamais l'esclavage de Rome!
> Périsse mon amour, périsse mon espoir,
> Plutôt que de ma main parte un crime si noir! (886 ff.)

What now has created his dilemma is simply to have discovered how generous and trusting his master is.

His agony is pathetically depicted, and we can pity him; but his solution when he fails to convert Emilie to his sentiments, though it may be *généreux*, would be sadly inadequate: to kill Auguste, and himself afterwards (1062 ff.).

Neither Cinna nor Maxime had made public their love for Emilie. Jealousy could easily produce in Maxime resentment, and disbelief in all Cinna's disinterestedness:

> Et c'est pour l'acquérir qu'il nous fait conspirer. (712)
>
> Je pense servir Rome, et je sers mon rival. (720)

Maxime is quite easily tempted to betray the plot by a freedman (and we shall meet the scorn and hatred of freedmen – ex-slaves – again in Martian of *Othon*). So doing he lets Cinna off his dilemma and leaves him free to take up a role which suits him better, that of convicted plotter, confessing and defending his design.

But Maxime's betrayal is a turning-point, and brings us to the second half of the tragedy, in which Auguste seizes the central role. We saw this broken-backed construction in *Horace*, and I suggested (though of course the story there leaves no alternative) that it served Corneille's desire to take the reader or audience right round his situation and show it from every side. A technical explanation would be that Corneille had not yet mastered the art of running the sub-plot or *épisode* parallel with the main action, starting it as nearly as possible at the same time and making its events coincide with the others: they will of course end at the same moment, one contributing to the other.[14] In *Polyeucte* the problem will have been solved. Sévère arrives the moment Polyeucte has received baptism: coincidence is very often the price of keeping the Unity of Time.

Auguste learns of the plot and has his scene of agonized self-questioning (IV. 2), the equivalent of the sleepless night in Seneca's account. He recalls all the crimes we have heard of from Cinna's lips, and our image of him darkens again correspondingly. It has more in common with the picture Cinna had given to the conspirators, than with that of the seemingly serene but world-weary sage we saw in Act II. Herland has forced down his pan of the balance against Cinna's, in order to make more of the great moral ascent the emperor makes in the denouement. He goes rather too far – Auguste is not quite comparable with Macbeth, as Herland later admitted.[15]

As in Seneca, Livie comes in with her suggestion of trying clemency. And here we find the first indication that Corneille has decided to borrow Seneca's material only to rewrite it. His Auguste rejects the advice gruffly; and anger, remorse and lassitude prevent him from coming to any decision.

The denouement is thus a triumph of the art of suspense. Cinna is pinned down on his seat and has to endure, speechless, the calm but scathing revelation of his crime and description of his unworthiness (V. 1). Thus far, as in Seneca; but Corneille interrupts the action with the sudden introduction of Emilie, who comes to claim her part in the punishment; and Auguste stops short; we do not know, nor probably does he, what he will do next. (He is reduced to silence, but not by astonishment, for he has to listen to important speeches – Emilie's confession, and the *assaut de générosité* in which each conspirator tries to claim all the guilt and exonerates the other [V. 2]). His own reactions, when they come, are designed by Corneille to keep us in suspense (the art of the *quiproquo* comes in useful here), Auguste's aim seems to be to delay his decision and yet give some indication of a stern judicial attitude. Cinna has been told to choose his own punishment (1561). To the couple he says:

> Oui, je vous unirai, couple ingrat et perfide,
> Et plus mon ennemi qu'Antoine ni Lépide,
> Oui, je vous unirai, puisque vous le voulez:
> Il faut bien satisfaire aux feux dont vous brûlez,
> Et que tout l'univers, sachant ce qui m'anime,
> S'étonne du supplice aussi bien que du crime. (1657 ff.)

At last Maxime appears, greeted with joy, and adds the last straw. His confession of treachery gives rise to that gloriously dramatic and emotional, mysteriously unexplained, outburst of clemency which would, according to Seneca, have followed, cold, upon Cinna's humiliation. Its warmth gains the culprits as it gains us (for surely few can read this scene without emotion) – Emilie capitulates first, showing a nature responsive to *générosité*; Cinna has to follow after, for she must release him from the oath he would not break.

Many explanations have been given for this *coup de théâtre*, most of them acceptable (not all; not Napoleon's, which reveals his moral limitations). The first is that it *is* a *coup de théâtre*, an act, spontaneous and characteristic of his better nature, but unexpected, above all by himself. Or, he reaches the highest achievement commended by the stoic philosophy, the mastery of self; or he abolishes rancour and desire of revenge in his enemies by an example which is noble, and even courageous (for he courts renewed violence if it fails); or he remembers Livie's utilitarian arguments which he had brushed aside. But Corneille shows his genius in not trying to explain it and by letting its effect operate. The bullying tone of Auguste, borrowed from Seneca's account, is forgotten by all, himself included. Herland has spoken (op. cit.) of divine grace, described it is true in a pagan context, but indicating a Providence which, through appointed monarchs (the Divine Right of Kings) takes care of the course of the world. Herland may well be right; some such intention is clear in the repeated references to inspiration – Auguste hopes for guidance (1258), Emilie receives mysterious intimations (1293 ff.), Livie announces a prophetic revelation (1753) which conveniently opens the curtain on a smiling future. Corneille will not scruple to invent such divine revelations even in the martyr tragedy *Theodore*: his doctrine is presumably that since martyrologies recount such things we know they *can* happen and they are therefore not *invraisemblables*; and monarchies being under Divine guidance, as he and his age mostly believed, it is credible that interventions should occur in favour of the greatest (then) of world powers.

This is the first tragedy in French literary history to end happily. The theoretical question of the legitimacy of such a thing had just been settled[16] and Corneille had noticed that Greek usage, and the *Poetics*, freely admit it. For him it clearly suffices that the 'péril' which defined the Unity of Action (p.119) should be sufficiently grave to excite the tragic emotions; and the denouement dramatically adequate, not merely by winding up the situation and removing all apprehension, but by exhibiting acts of heroic virtue.

Corneille must have been fully satisfied with the reaction of his audience; we shall see him bring about the denouement by an act of magnanimous clemency several times again, though never in quite the same moral circumstances; rather as a statesmanlike act of real heroism involving renunciation of vengeance or some other good and founding a reconciliation – as in *Pertharite* (perhaps), *Nicomède* and *Agésilas*.

***Polyeucte*: the hero as martyr**

> On voit mal comment une pièce destinée à célébrer l'avènement de Dieu et son empire sur l'homme se raccorderait au reste d'une œuvre orientée vers l'exaltation du Moi et des vertus de l'orgueil.

So writes S. Doubrovski,[17] begging two important questions. In the first place, not everyone will recognize his description of the metaphysical atmosphere in which Corneille's earlier heroes had lived and breathed. In the second, *Polyeucte* is not, as Doubrovski feels obliged to assume, a sermon, nor a treatise nor an allegory about Christian belief or Christian life, any more than *Le Cid* is propaganda (Doubrovski's word) for, or instruction in, the Spanish code of honour, or *Horace* for patriotism. Polyeucte is not the pattern held up for every Christian who loves his wife; Corneille is not saying that love is a temptation of the devil for all such. Polyeucte is unpopular with many of the opposite sex, like Horace, because of the way he treats his wife. A fanatic? perhaps; a man of passionate and exclusive convictions – a recent convert convinced that he has a special call to martyrdom, whose wife is not convinced. A special, painful, extreme case, which the playwright, who seeks extremes, has seized upon eagerly. Nor is it unreal – it could happen today; love tending to weaken the resolution of a hero – that is a theme we shall often meet again.

We need not attribute these emotions to the playwright. His Christianity is well known; sincere, we believe, but sober. It may seem curious that he would have thought of producing a religious play; they were only just coming back into a certain favour. Perhaps he wanted to try the effect of a surprise. What he has given us is not a call to discipleship, but a spectacle of conflict, a study, not cool but intensely and sympathetically imagined, of the conflicting forces he has called into action – like Giotto painting St Francis.

Polyeucte's love is strong, and recent; and he sees it as a temptation, as indeed it is, when Pauline comes to beg him to recant: she is ranging herself with the Tempter.

Cléon Pauline vous demande.
P. O présence, ô combat que surtout j'appréhende!
Félix, dans la prison j'ai triomphé de toi,
J'ai ri de ta menace, et t'ai vu sans effroi:
Tu prends pour t'en venger de plus puissantes armes;
Je craignais beaucoup moins tes bourreaux que ses larmes.
Seigneur, qui vois ici les périls que je cours,
En ce pressant besoin redouble ton secours. (1082 ff.)

Her love is one of the

flatteuses voluptés,
Honteux attachements de la chair et du monde, (1106 f.)

and he brings himself to say:

Et je ne regarde Pauline
Que comme un obstacle à mon bien. (1143 f.)

It seems a weakness in the depiction of this figure that he is hardly ever shown trying to explain to anybody the religion forwhich he is about to die. His first sermon, as reported by Stratonice, deals only with the unique power of God. With Félix, though he has already unmasked his father-in-law's pretended desire to learn and embrace Christianity (1523 ff., 1568 ff.), he does give a quite acceptable account of his creed, even an allusion to the doctrine of the Mass – but it comes very late in the action;

Je n'adore qu'un Dieu, maître de l'univers,
Sous qui tremblent le ciel, la terre, et les enfers,
Un Dieu qui, nous aimant d'une amour infinie,
Voulut mourir pour nous avec ignominie,
Et qui par un effort de cet excès d'amour,
Veut pour nous en victime être offert chaque jour.
Mais j'ai tort d'en parler à qui ne peut m'entendre. (1657 ff.)

but then he returns to his oft-repeated attacks on the vices attributed to the pagan divinities. And to his beloved Pauline he vouchsafes no teaching:

Si vous pouviez comprendre et le peu qu'est la vie,
Et de quelles douceurs cette mort est suivie!
Mais que sert de parler de ces trésors cachés
A des esprits que Dieu n'a pas encor touchés? (1231 ff.)

Faith is a gift of grace, 'un don du ciel, et non de la raison' (1554); and he believes it will come with his intercession after his death (1263 f.). It has to be remembered that *Polyeucte* is a play for the stage, where preaching was not welcomed and was not considered very appropriate: it is in fact surprising to find the martyr as well-versed in his belief as he is, and so ready to speak of it. It is clear too that at the moment when he speaks he has no hope of persuading her: he knows that she has come to appeal to him, full of her wifely task of dissuading him from his voluntary death, and her sense of duty would stop her ears to anything he might say. He is not lacking in affection, though he masks it by deliberate hardness:

Je vous l'ai déjà dit, et vous le dis encore,
Vivez avec Sévère ou mourez avec moi. (1608 f.)

Ne suivez point mes pas ou quittez vos erreurs. (1682)

He even makes plans – which must be discussed later – for her happiness 'au monde' if the 'bienheureux moment' (1277) of her conversion should come late, or never.

Polyeucte aspires 'à la gloire'; and this unfortunate word, with its wealth of equivocations, has done him great disservice. S. Doubrovski, blinded also by his concept of the 'projet de Maîtrise', the hero's aspiration to achieve liberty by putting down every competitor, goes so far as to entitle one of his chapters 'Polyeucte, ou la conquête de Dieu'.

The confusion has arisen, perhaps, because the theorists of 'l'Ethique de la Gloire' have run together the basic idea of *fame* and the acts or qualities that may win fame according to the ethics of a class or an era. In Polyeucte's mouth it does not even mean *fame*. It is only right to remember that 'glory' (*gloria, gloire*) has a far longer history in Judaeo-Christian religion than in feudal culture: it is the attribute and the environment of God himself, to which, in the New Testament, he admits his faithful servants as to a recompense that scripture often encourages them to hope for and desire. This is the glory Polyeucte hopes to win, where he believes his comrade Néarque awaits him (1522); this is how we must understand him when he speaks, as he (quite rarely) does, of his aspirations:

J'ai de l'ambition, mais plus noble et plus belle
[than the earthly status of which Pauline reminds him]:
Cette grandeur périt, j'en veux une immortelle,
Un bonheur assuré, sans mesure et sans fin. (1191 ff.)

But is it true that Corneille has let his sense of heroism destroy the true character of his religion? It has been claimed that Polyeucte is too boastful and self-confident to be a true Christian. But is he?

Nearque Qui n'appréhende rien présume trop de soi.
P. J'attends tout de sa grâce et rien de ma faiblesse.
(680–1)

This is the purest orthodoxy. Or what of this?

Allons, mon cher Néarque, allons aux yeux des hommes,
Braver l'idolâtrie, et montrer qui nous sommes. (645 f.)

What are they to show themselves? Heroes, or martyrs? Simply worshippers of the true God. Divine grace has made his heroic choice easier, preceded as it has been by the test of his zeal, the temptation to yield to Pauline and delay the day of the baptism (I. 1).

As Polyeucte prepares to go and be baptized, Pauline tries to hold him back – she has had a dream appearing to forbode calamity (a dream sent by God, in whom she does not believe? And for what purpose? Corneille does not tell us, and perhaps could not. It may be just one of the traditional 'properties' of tragedy). But why does Polyeucte not explain at once why he must go? It would seem natural to. No doubt he realized that he would spoil his honeymoon by one of the disputes that were certain to come; but it seems quite unwise and cowardly to shirk it, since it must come some time. This is an awkwardness in the action that is at least useful in that it prepares for the argument with Néarque about delaying, which reveals a good deal of the convert's state of mind. But what are we to say of the astonishing inconsistency, or insincerity, he shows on his return (II. 4)? There is still no word of his conversion to the detested sect; instead he reassures his wife – all is well, her fears were ill-founded. Then (because of the coming of Sévère, of whom more later) he is summoned to attend a thanksgiving sacrifice. He invites her to come: 'Y venez-vous, Madame?' (629). She is afraid because Sévère has appeared in the dream, and has a grudge against her husband. Polyeucte reassures her again:

> Allez, tout son crédit n'a rien que j'appréhende,
> Et comme je connais sa générosité
> Nous ne nous combattrons que de civilité. (634 ff.)

Yet immediately afterwards he makes it clear to Néarque that he intends to create one tremendous scandal by smashing idols and proclaiming his faith. Was it to witness this that he wanted to bring his wife? Were his reassurances false?

Certainly the episode has dramatic value. Polyeucte's unexpected willingness to go to the temple is comparable with Cinna's unexpected championship of the principle of monarchy in the council scene; and the scene later where Polyeucte explains his intention to the half-reluctant Néarque provides a fine surprise. But the same critic who has seen a hint of divine inspiration in Auguste's unexplained decision to show clemency (p. 33) proposes with greater plausibility, in this play where the spirit of Christianity is so rarely absent, to think that in the very moment when he is as it were challenged to go to the temple Polyeucte is inspired to go and make his demonstration, scarcely conscious that he is being inconsistent.[18] It may quite well be so; but Corneille might have explained more carefully.

It is high time to speak of Sévère. This character, the pure invention of Corneille (as far as we know), comes close to attracting too much interest to the sub-plot built around himself and Pauline. Many of Corneille's public preferred it to the story of Polyeucte's martyrdom; many perhaps still do. It can hardly be necessary to recall the outline of this pathetic and purely secular action – how the Roman 'knight' had loved Pauline in Rome and been rejected by her ambitious father, had gone off to the wars in despair and was believed dead (which was when Pauline, arriving in Armenia, accepted marriage to the nobleman Polyeucte); but returned alive and covered in glory, the favourite of the emperor whose life he had saved in a battle; and now arrived most inopportunely to preside at a religious thanksgiving ceremony, hoping to see Pauline but placing her, who has tried to forget him but not successfully enough, in an agonizing conflict of duties. Her father forces her to see Sévère, hoping somehow to placate the anger he believes the rejected suitor must still bear him. With great nobility she confesses to him her present marriage and her past love, which must be blotted out. When her husband has proclaimed himself a Christian and is awaiting death, she calls on Sévère to work against his own hopes and use his influence to try to save him.

This is a long way from the story told by O. Nadal.[19] He has let himself be influenced by the idea of this 'Ethique de la Gloire' which he has built up for himself, out of generalizations I think unwarranted (since he has already had to admit that there are exceptions) in virtue of which he thinks that members of a certain social class felt it imperative to sacrifice everything to their *gloire* – which often meant in plain words, to their social aggrandizement, and recognized no other form of duty. Such a feeling did operate and was understood – witness don Alvar of *Don Sanche* and the later Domitie of *Tite et Bérénice*. But Pauline denies feeling this. She tells Sévère:

Si le ciel en mon choix eût mis mon hyménée,
A vos seules vertus je me serais donnée,
Et toute la rigueur de votre premier sort
Contre votre mérite eût fait un vain effort.
Je découvrais en vous d'assez illustres marques

Pour vous préférer même aux plus heureux monarques,
(465 ff.)

At Rome, according to Nadal, 'au nom de la Gloire. Pauline a refusé de s'allier à l'obscur chevalier Sévère'. Quite amicably and quietly. 'Aucun désaccord entre les amants et Félix; . . . . le plus dur effort eût été pour eux de vaincre l'espoir de la Gloire.' The marriage she later submits to with Polyeucte 'est dans l'ordre . . . . Il satisfait pleinement cette passion de la grandeur et de la gloire . . . Ce fut aussi pour elle un "devoir" d'aimer Polyeucte, mais il faut bien entendre ce mot. Il s'agit d'une obligation qui n'a coûté aucun effort à Pauline puisqu'elle allait dans le sens de son idéal.'

Let us hear her again.

[Sévère] possédait mon cœur, mes désirs, ma pensée,
Je ne lui cachais point combien d'étais blessée.
Nous soupirions ensemble et pleurions nos malheurs.
Mais au lieu d'espérance, il n'avait que des pleurs,
Et malgré des soupirs si doux, si favorables,
Mon père et mon devoir étaient inexorables. (197 ff.)

Et moi, comme à son lit je me vis destinée,
Je *donnai par devoir* à son affection
Tout *ce que l'autre avait par inclination.* (214 ff.)

One may think that in one respect she was too much of a slave to the conventions of her day and her class – in the high value she placed on the duty of obedience to that odious father of hers. But after all, Sévère having disappeared, what else was she to do?

Nadal is entitled to stress that she believes she has transferred her love successfully and peacefully, but not to suppress the lines which confess the contrary, and not to play down her fear of facing Sévère again: 'Le "charme" qui emporte Pauline vers Sévère est cette attraction même qu'exercent sur elle le prestige du héros, sa renommée, ses actions triomphales. Ce ne sont ni la personne de Sévère, ni son amour . . . Le mouvement de Pauline vers Sévère est non pas un retour inspiré par une tendresse encore vivante ou par le souvenir d'une blessure mal fermée, mais exactement l'accomplissement d'un devoir . . . Pauline vient trouver Sévère en service commandé.' Of course, and hence the shuddering, horrified revolt:

Moi, Moi! que je revoie un si puissant vainqueur,
Et m'expose à des yeux qui me percent le cœur!
Mon père, ju suis femme, et je sais ma faiblesse,
Je sens déjà mon cœur qui pour lui s'intéresse,
Et poussera sans doute, en dépit da ma foi,
Quelque soupir indigne et de vous et de moi.
Je ne le verrai point. (339 ff.)

We can choose to believe either Pauline or Nadal. There are, it is true, characters in Corneille whose words we cannot believe; but the careful reader takes note of them, and of the indication of the obvious motive which is there to guide the reader who is willing to be guided. This 'reading' is too careful by half. Pauline, speaking to confidant, father or even to Sévère, is not to be doubted that way. She is the victim of the mass of a priori generalizations the critic has accumulated about *gloire*; it does not constitute a legitimate hypothesis, for he has been obliged to make exceptions for Chimène and Camille: why not for Pauline? According to her, the old love has been reawakened – or almost – and she has a dreadful fight of it.

She and Sévère do make much play with the words *gloire* and *devoir* – more than Polyeucte or Néarque. We shall do well to remind ourselves of the use made of the words *honour* or *reputation* by English writers of an earlier generation; and to recall that at that time a woman's honour consisted in avoiding 'dishonour'; and also to notice that the words *honourable, dishonourable*, are still current but have almost lost their connection with honour.

When Sévère says to Pauline: 'Je veux mourir des miens [de mes maux], aimez-en la mémoire,' and she replies: 'Je veux guérir des miens, ils souilleraient ma gloire,' (549 ff.) no one thinks she has any intention that the world shall know of her temptations or her struggles.

Corneille seems to have seen her, and her episode, as symmetrical to her husband and his more tragic adventure. She is a fanatic too, a fanatic of duty, and on the most human levels; duty to father (surely overdone, now she is legally under her husband's authority?) and to her husband, whom she must endeavour to serve by undermining his beliefs – and this of course is why Polyeucte fears her so much and treats her so roughly.

In playing down Pauline's repugnance to meeting her former lover,

Nadal seems to be trying to avoid the picture of the woman in love with two men, and show her in unbroken union with her husband and worthy to be drawn up by him and with him into the perfect union in God. (But why would the martyr to duty be less worthy?) So at least I understand his argument (op. cit., 205), which he backs with no specific references to the play, apart from the scenes that tell of the wife's conversion.

I find Pauline the stronger witness.

After the second pathetic scene between husband and wife, comes the episode (IV. 4) that most critics greet with an embarrassed smile. Here is a writer so simple-minded, so unversed in the ways of the world, that he can expect to get away with showing a husband trying to bestow on a rival the wife he has loved and who loves him – it is almost shocking in its ignorance of human nature. I believe that Corneille knew exactly what he was doing: that he had correctly calculated the motives that should reign in a perfectly regenerated human being, and coolly produced the episode, intending by the clash between two norms of conduct to produce a thrill of surprise, which might please after the first shock – or might offend. We shall see another such case, in *Pertharite*. The martyr has extinguished love, sexual love, for his wife because it is a temptation: charity, with compassion and tender considerateness, is not dead and prompts him to try to encourage her to live 'heureuse au monde', once freed by his death, and Sévère to consider that the barrier has been removed between the two of them. He leaves them speechless. Sévère breaks the silence with banal expressions of astonishment: Pauline, fanatical as ever, denies the possibility of love between them (it is the official attitude of Chimène, but this time deadly earnest), and demands that her lover should do all he can to save the husband – a paradox there also.

The denouement, with two miraculous conversions following the two martyrdoms, is in keeping with the play – a *tragédie heureuse* once again; Corneille has said that it would have been ridiculous to venture such an ending in the atmosphere of savage hatred that reigned in his later tragedy *Théodore*; he has made it seem fitting here. But such conversions can take place by the action of divine grace at the intercession of a martyr: I take it that all theologians will agree; *vraisemblance* therefore is safe. Félix is such a mean-souled creature that his salvation is hard to accept – but it will do good, because it means a temporary lull in the local persecution. Sévère will intercede with the emperor, but is not converted. This *parfait honnête homme*, coolly impartial in all his attitudes, is not, Corneille realizes, a very likely subject. 'Peut-être qu'un jour' (1797) something may happen.

We admire his calm and firm statement of sympathetic toleration for all religions, a fitting conclusion to a martyr-play:

> J'approuve cependant que chacun ait ses Dieux,
> Qu'il les serve à sa mode, et sans peur de la peine.
>
> (1798 f.)

– but we rarely reflect that, in the general form Corneille has given it, it is a revolutionary principle that few, in the France of his day, would have been prepared to accept, and very few to proclaim. It is true that this is only a pagan advocating tolerance towards Christians, which is much more acceptable than if the case had been reversed; but once again, as in the unconscious pacifism of *Horace*, we see how Corneille's exploration of general principles can take him much further than he knows or, probably, wishes.[20]

Diverse as may be the characters, the actions and the themes in the plays of the Tetralogy, what unites them – and them perhaps alone in Corneille's work – is that they are all based on dilemmas. The dilemmas are not between good and bad, as in many tragicomedies like *L'Amour tyrannique* by Scudéry; a thoroughly unproductive opposition, for if we are given a hero who is virtuous he will not hesitate, and the effect will be wasted – but between two goods, of a different order, where the priorities are uncertain, but have to be fixed. The conflicts are grave, they can be seen as exemplary.

The heroes are virtuous; they are *généreux* (passionately devoted to honour), but not faultless models: only Rodrigue is shown as entirely in the right – nor is anyone (if we except Maxime and Félix) entirely in the wrong. Here lies part of the greatness of the Tetralogy. (Polyeucte, though Corneille calls him a 'personne tout-à-fait vertueuse', is not the same thing; we have to wait for César in *Pompée* to find a frigid figure of effortless, infallible virtue.)

Starobinski[21] has depicted the Cornelian hero as a dazzling figure calling forth from the world the acclaim in which he basks; but we are entitled to ask which hero he is thinking of (Horace of Act II perhaps; or Nicomède?) In the tetralogy, the heroes are as unlike each other as are their situations. Rodrigue is impeccable, Chimène is touching by her comparative frailty – she has what the poet calls two 'faux pas' or 'glissades' in which she allows her real desire to be seen; Cinna is not in the least idealized; Emilie, as rigid as he is impressionable, is forced in the end to condemn her own resolution; Auguste makes a brilliant conquest of magnanimity, but a conquest late and painfully achieved; *Polyeucte* is not alone a legend of a tough voluntary martyr, but the touching story of a woman twice and blamelessly in love. But Horace, always quoted as the typical Cornelian hero, ends under the condemnation of all in Act IV. I have already hinted that I think this tragedy of wartime patriotism to be the most sensitive study of the different ways in which this problem can be faced that has ever, perhaps, been written.

What links this group of tragedies and distinguishes it from others is the fact that the questions in them are moral problems. Heroism, here, is about virtue; it will not be, later. Corneille of course never tried to teach morality; but the problems he makes his *glorieux* and *généreux* heroes face can be worded in terms of ethics. This is one of the things that gives the Tetralogy its great value; elsewhere Corneille will proclaim that 'la bonté des mœurs' which the *Poetics* demands does not refer to moral standards but is an aesthetic quality: it remains that we find it very hard to identify ourselves with a Medea or a Cléopâtre (in *Rodogune*) or even the cold *politiques* of so many plays. 'We only feel pity for people like ourselves.'

It could be objected that we very rarely find ourselves in the position of having to avenge a father and lose a mistress, or to win glory at the cost of our nearest affections, or to pardon a conspirator, or even to smash a statue. And Corneille has perhaps not always played quite fair: for his problems and solutions are not entirely in accordance with the principles of the most exalted morality, with those of Christianity which we must presume he accepted himself – duels and revenge, and even 'temerarious zeal' like that of Polyeucte, had all been condemned. But the way in which his characters speak of their motives – in general terms – makes it easy to take their values as real: loyalty, justice, duty whatever it may be, the rights of the individual or the claims of the city, the claims of this world or those of the next.

These high themes are no longer prominent after *Polyeucte*. *La Mort de Pompée* continues them in a sense, in that it shows the bankruptcy of 'Machiavellian' unscrupulousness, but it is the Machiavellians who debate, who plot and struggle. Cornélie strikes a histrionic pose which will cost her nothing; César is serene, self-confident and some of his actions are on the physical plane alone, the plane which Corneille had decided is of less importance. (The thing that interests us about him is the doubt cast by an eyewitness on his sincerity.) In *Rodogune* the two sons of the murderous queen resist her for moral reasons – they are perhaps the last Cornelian characters to interest us in doing so – but the prominent character in that play is the queen, and the prominent motive her wicked lust for power – a *héroïne en mal* like Médée, as Corneille points out.

Characters will continue to be, for instance, magnanimous in offering reconciliation, and several fine denouements are obtained thereby; but such heroes are of lesser moral stature – Nicomède, courageous but only in defence of the rights of Kings, the usurper Grimoald, whose enemies think him the more dangerous because of his evident virtues, Pompée (in *Sertorius*), the undignified temporiser. Interest passes to the violent defenders of what they claim as their rights, and depends on mystery and suspense; and later, with or after *Oedipe*, to the calculations and ambitions of leaders of factions, realists and realistically depicted – the seamy side of 'l'Ethique de la Gloire', the problem of the limits set to virtue in public life; a second manner which Corneille adopts and changes only for the sombre abnegations of his last plays.

When Corneille forsook the theme of idealized heroism, did he realize what a violent *coup de barre* he was making? and did his admirers feel it? It would seem not. In modern eyes it is the most abrupt departure he ever took; but his prefaces and *Examens* never allude to it. He writes as if *Pompée*, *Oedipe* or *Othon* were distinguished by the same merits as his greatest works; and he can discuss the 'constitution assez extraordinaire' of *Nicomède*, which we see as much closer to the older formula.

It is hard to decide whether he was trying to pass off wares of a different quality, or whether he saw in the moral dilemma only a source of dramatic pleasure like the others, which he had used to advantage, worn out and thrown away.

III
The Pressure Falls

La Mort de Pompée: a feeble imitation

History closes the period of the Tetralogy with a date that appears to be significant, though it is not easy to see what it signifies. Between *Polyeucte* and *Pompée* (it is hard to date the *composition* of a play, but this seems to be the chronology) comes the death of Richelieu – the man who had presided over the birth and the growth, over eighteen years, of the popular, regular, commercial, professional theatre in Paris; and this includes the whole of Corneille's career so far. We know the theory[1] which attributes a good deal of the heroism, of the specific Cornelian *Sublime*, in the Tetralogy to the direct influence of the cardinal, who was conducting a propaganda campaign in favour of a fairly totalitarian form of patriotism through the writers he was subsidizing (but not the playwrights). Corneille had been his pensioner since 1635. But the only direct evidence that the poet accepted such a mandate is his dedication of *Horace* to Richelieu.

> Certes, Monseigneur, ce changement visible qu'on remarque en mes ouvrages depuis que j'ai l'honneur d'être à V.E., qu'est-ce autre chose qu'un effet des grandes idées qu'elle m'inspire quand elle daigne souffrir que je lui rende mes devoirs?

Corneille must have been glad to let the world know of his confidential talks with the cardinal, and delighted to talk to a real minister about real concerns of state; but there must be flattery in his words, and there may very well be irony[2] – 'grandes idées' is an expression very capable of ambiguity; and even *Horace*, to say nothing of the tragedies that followed, is by no means a piece of straight propaganda for single-minded patriotism; and the other two are nothing of the kind.

What is certain is that with Richelieu's disappearance the tone does change. The steam has gone out of the heroism that marked the Tetralogy, or so I feel at least. The Romans are still there in *Pompée*,[3] but they have it easy: Caesar faces only physical danger, there are no moral conflicts. That bore Cornélie faces no danger at all, and her defiance is empty words. Our interest is directed to the wicked Egyptians, because they do the plotting and the action. No drama is extracted from strictly moral issues as such, as it had been before (except when César disapproves of assassination), nor, I think, will it ever be again in Corneille. Only one figure is given heroic stature, and he never appears, dying offshore before Act II.[4]

No one would like to think that the sublimities of the poet's greatest period had been created without conviction, to be dropped as soon as the pay stopped. Let us rather suppose, what is equally possible, that Richelieu had perhaps helped him to find that rich vein, but that the vein had now been worked out – there is some truth in the old formula of the progression from duty to family, to national claims, to the ideal state, to God – and it was time to change to something else. But he was not sure what.

It is not easy to find consistency of purpose, or unity of theme, in the next period of his work. The decade 1642–52 shows only one firm decision on Corneille's part – to turn his back on what we tend to think are his supreme qualities.

So while waiting for new inspiration he turned, not for the first or the last time, to another genre; this time, back to comedy. It is not part of this study to describe *Le Menteur* or its *Suite*. We may assume that their effect was to increase even further Corneille's interest in plot (a feature which had arisen first in comedy) – in the mechanisms by which a dramatist can control or propel his action in the direction he wishes. Interest in plot-mechanics seems in fact to be what characterizes the next pair of tragedies I shall treat. (For, in looking for a pattern in which to group what follows, the best seemed to me to be to see it as consisting of two pairs of brilliant works, interspersed with relative failures.)

Théodore, vierge et martyre: a failure

But first we must find room to speak of *Théodore*, which occupies the years 1644–47 with *Rodogune* and *Héraclius*; it is not certain that it precedes *Héraclius*; but it would be quite like Corneille to run away from a successful new play (as *Rodogune* was) and attempt to surprise his public with a novelty (as he did with *Clitandre*, or *Horace*). If he hoped to succeed with this rather crude play of cruelty and violence, he deserved to fail; and he failed, for the first time. He refused to appeal against his failure, but found it convenient to attribute it to an episode involving prostitution – convenient, because a Church Father, St Ambrose, had told that story and thought it edifying.

The animosity that leads to the death of Théodore and two other people is caused, not by religion, but by a mother's fury on account of a daughter (whom we never see, and never need to) who does nothing but die, literally, for love (a thing no other character of Corneille is known to do). She loves her mother's stepson Placide and he is indifferent to her; they have been betrothed but he sees this, rightly, as a part of his stepmother's tyranny over the household (she is sister of the emperor's favourite, and lets father and son know it). But surely murderous hatred was never assigned a pettier or feebler motive. This theme is most incongruously combined with a story of Christian martyrdom: the mother determines to destroy Théodore, whom Placide loves; but Théodore rejects him, and also another suitor Didyme for whom she has more inclination. She is, it turns out, a Christian (we are in the times following Diocletian's persecution) and has taken a vow of virginity. This makes her, as Corneille admits in his *Examen*, a passionless character, 'un Terme qui n'a ni jambes ni bras'. Her punishment – by prostitution, in order to attack her by what is dearer to her than life – and her rescue by Didyme, fill the middle part of the play. Théodore and Didyme (who is also a Christian) squabble rather unedifyingly over their martyr's palm, in an *assaut de générosité* (V. 5) recalling that of Emile and Cinna. Two murders, off stage – those of the martyrs, who are stabbed in revenge, not executed – and two suicides on, round off the proceedings. The wicked mother has political influence, and this brings this element into the plot; she might be allowed to join the ranks of Corneille's wicked heroines. Her craven and subservient husband Valens is viler than Felix and may prefigure Prusias. Otherwise I cannot fit this ill-conceived piece into the sequence at all. Of the principal characters only Valens is permitted to get away with his life, and his cannot be called a happy ending, unless because he is rid of an insufferable wife.

Rodogune and *Héraclius*: experiments in plot

The first brilliant pair of plays is of course *Rodogune* and *Héraclius* – brilliant for the building-up of climax; tragedies of situation or of intrigue, we may say, borrowing terms belonging normally to comedy (but what they really betoken is the close presence of tragicomedy). Anyone who analyses the story-lines will find they have grown much longer than in the tragedies that precede.

Théodore had had some attachments with history. *Rodogune* and *Héraclius* represent the highest point of the disdain which Corneille was sometimes capable of showing for that historical authority which at other times he loved to claim. In the first of the two plays, as he says himself, what he had done was to 'feindre un sujet entier sous des noms véritables'. The second he says is 'une hardie entreprise sur l'histoire'.

Perhaps the fact that they are entirely invented is the reason why the expositions have to be rather laborious, as they are. Both depend on a secret concerning a birth, an idea which comes, of course, from comedy and tragicomedy.

In *Rodogune* it is the order of births which is kept secret. In *Héraclius* it is the identity of a child which has been, not once, but twice exchanged for another. The secret of *Rodogune* is one deliberately kept by the wicked queen Cléopâtre of Syria (nothing to do with Cleopatra of Egypt), who wishes thereby to keep a hold on the throne. We never know which of two twin sons was born first and, as Corneille says, given the data of the play, if we were told, there is only the Queen who could tell us, and we should not believe her after all she has done and said. The secret (implausible though it is) gives Corneille the means to control and to balance the events in his action. He gives us two brothers, both in love with the same woman, a foreign princess who has been sent to marry the (undisclosed) heir and seal a peace treaty, who loves one but we are not told at this stage which – the princess Rodogune keeps her secret.

The mother tells them that she will give the succession, not to the one who is the firstborn, but the one who will please her by killing this princess in whom she sees a rival. Neither of them is going to do it. As a riposte the Princess Rodogune (though she later says she never expected to be obeyed) says she will marry the one who will kill his own mother to please her, in revenge for his father – a complicated history which I will try not to have to go into.

Later the mother tries to tempt one son to kill the other. (Corneille lets them both go without a name for two whole acts – we never know which is which, until one retires from the struggle and their paths diverge.)

In the end, since she cannot bring them to do her will, the Queen would like both of them to die. One does, and the last Act is a finely tuned balance in which the surviving son, on the point of marrying his Rodogune, is uncertain whether the death of his brother was caused by the woman he loves or the mother he tries to respect.

The two brothers are rather characterless – they cannot, of course, do much; Corneille has arranged for them to be trapped in a balance of motives just like Othon later, just like Bajazet in Racine. The motive they are asked to follow is vengeance, which on neither side is a sincere motive and lacks conviction anyway – it is a motive of tragicomedy. If they kill Rodogune it would be because she had been married, almost but not quite, to their father and turned him against his own country. If they killed their mother it would be because she was guilty of that father's death; as indeed she was – but it was a father they had never known. His part in the past is an awkward feature, for he had been their own rival in love. But they have no real *moral* problem to face and solve, to give them heroic status. Their actions are extremely moral, their refusals to commit immoral actions are very decided. The lack of interesting moral questions is a thing that is a necessary compensation for the excitement and complication of the plot: you can't have everything at the same time.

The women's characters have also been questioned. They lack perhaps naturalness; they, too, act for the sake of a well-contrived plot. At least, however, the wicked queen is wicked to the point of showing a certain 'grandeur d'âme', as Corneille himself pleads in his *Premier Discours*, which has 'quelque chose de si haut, qu'en même temps qu'on déteste ses actions on admire la source dont elles partent', and this in fact is the highest merit of the play; unless higher still comes that stagecraft which has produced the excitement, the successive *coups de théâtre*. This is the way Corneille himself praises himself in his *Examen*:

> Je veux bien laisser chacun en liberté de ses sentiments, mais certainement on peut dire que mes autres pièces ont peu d'avantages qui ne se rencontrent en celle-ci. Elle a tout ensemble la beauté du sujet, la nouveauté des fictions, la force des vers, la facilité de l'expression, la solidité du raisonnement, la chaleur des passions, les tendresses de l'amour et de l'amitié; et cet heureux assemblage est ménagé de sorte qu'elle s'élève d'acte en acte. Le second passe le premier, le troisième est au-dessus du second, et le dernier l'emporte sur tous les autres. L'action est une, grande, complète.

We meet no character of equal force in *Héraclius*, whereas *Héraclius* is the climax of all that Corneille has done in the matter of plot interest, of *embarras* as he calls them, created for the sake of a puzzle, for its own sake and not for the intrinsic interest really of what happens. I know no play of his which has a larger number of shifts of situation, of *péripéties* in the French sense of the word, unless it be *Othon*. Corneille himself says that of this play 'il s'est fait beaucoup de belles copies'; and it is true that, although the fear of incest is a motif which comes in certain tragicomedies earlier than this without the question of vengeance, all these *pseudos* that Mornet pointed out in a famous chapter on the sources of Racine are of later date, and must be considered as the inheritors of *Héraclius*.

Corneille himself thought that the denouement was a bit too clever. He says that

> Le stratagème d'Exupère, avec toute son industrie, a quelque chose un peu délicat, et d'une nature à ne se faire qu'au théâtre, où l'auteur est maître des événements qu'il tient dans sa main.

and till the last stratagem:

> toute sa conduite est de ces choses qu'il faut souffrir au théâtre, parce qu'elles ont un éclat dont la surprise éblouit, et qu'il ne ferait pas bon tirer en example pour conduire une action véritable sur leur plan. (*Examen*)

Voltaire has come up with a better solution in his *Remarques* on the play; which only shows really how great a movement of inventiveness Corneille launched with *Héraclius*.

The play is also, we remember, a kind of *reductio ad absurdum* of the problem of history versus *vraisemblance*. It is the text of the formula, which we all remember, 'que le sujet d'une belle tragédie doit n'être pas vraisemblable'.

It is in the preface of this play that Corneille proves that statement by Aristotle himself, who wants poets to use 'des événements extraordinaires qui se passent entre personnes proches, comme d'un père qui tue son fils' – 'ce qui, n'étant jamais vraisembable, doit avoir l'autorité de l'histoire ou de l'opinion commune pour être cru'.

True, for this mother of whom he is talking, who yields up her own son to save the son of the Emperor Mauritius, he comes up with historical warrant – except that history says Mauritius refused to let her; and it is Corneille's own (rather impudent) invention that she carried out another switch later. That was the bit of history which remained in what he has called 'une hardie entreprise'. So I suppose we are entitled to say that at the time this is what he thought was the best example he could provide of 'une belle tragédie' and of the 'événements extraordinaires' which Aristotle recommended as forming the only basis for the pathos of tragedy. He repeats the same thing in the *Examens* of 1660.

The situation is based on the fact that the Emperor of Constantinople, Mauritius, was killed with the whole of his family except for one daughter who was spared (Corneille says) as being useful to marry into the usurper's family later; but it was discovered that one son survived. He was saved, in the circumstances that have been discussed, by his foster-mother, but she later exchanged him once again with the son of the usurper Phocas himself. So the two young men are, when the play opens, wandering around with the wrong parentage. One has just been told who he is, and goes about uttering expressions of *double entendre*, which even the audience are not able to understand until they have seen the whole play through once.

It is fairly easy for us, with the training of the modern detective story and other puzzle exercises which Corneille's public did not have, to keep abreast – easier for us in fact with the text before us than for people in the theatre, because we must remember that the text gives the characters their real names: in the theatre we see them as they are believed at the moment to be. Corneille himself was rather proud of the complexity, the *embarras*, here.

> Le poème est si embarrassé qu'il demande une merveilleuse attention. J'ai vu de fort bons esprits, et des personnes des plus qualifiées de la cour, se plaindre de ce que sa représentation fatiguait autant l'esprit qu'une étude sérieuse. Elle n'a pas laissé de plaire, mais je crois qu'il l'a fallu voir plus d'une fois pour en remporter une entière intelligence.
>
> (*Examen*)

There is, of course, not only the question of being recognized as heir to the throne, there is the matter of vengeance. The usurper's son, whoever he turns out to be, owes a certain feeling of perfunctory respect to the acknowledgedly wicked man who is his father. The son of the murdered emperor owes his father a vengeance. And in a sense, if I can make myself clear, this duty of vengeance is purely ex officio. Relations in princely families in the seventeenth century were not such that a son could be expected to feel much real affection for his father even if he knew him. It depends on who you turn out to be, whether you have such a duty or not – a feature which the seventeenth century liked; we see it again later. We see it (inverted, as it were) in Rotrou's play *Cosroès* where the wife or mistress of Syroès thinks she is the daughter of the wicked queen whom Syroès will have to get rid of; and she stops him doing it. Then she discovers that there has been a switch in her case, and makes no further objection. The same obstacle does not exist. The ex officio duty occurs again in Quinault's *Astrate*.

There is also this business of the threat of incest which so titillated the seventeenth century. For there is this daughter, already mentioned, whom both the young men view with feelings which they take to be love, though she is in fact the sister of one of them. They listen, all who are involved in the family tangle listen in vain for 'la voix de la nature', 'la voix du sang', and it gives no certain answers in this play. All this then is a sort of debauchery of excitement which Corneille is exploiting and which, we have seen, was much admired and much imitated. Corneille himself came to condemn explicitly in the *Discours* of 1660 a practice which one would think he must have seen he was exploiting here; or not precisely, perhaps. What he says in his second dramaturgical *Discours* is that

> Quand [la découverte] ne se fait qu'après la mort de l'inconnu, la compassion qu'excitent les déplaisirs de celui qui le fait périr ne peut avoir grande étendue, puisqu'elle est reculée et renfermée dans la catastrophe. Mais lorsqu'on agit à visage découvert, et qu'on sait à qui on en veut, le combat des passions contre la nature, ou du devoir contre l'amour, occupe la meilleure partie du poème, et de là naissent les grandes et fortes émotions qui renouvellent à tous moments et redoublent la commisération. (B 41)

This is what he had done everywhere else. Here, he has introduced the complication that both the young men know that this tragic discovery may await them, but are uncertain whether it will. Out of this glorious *embarras* Corneille gets every foot of mileage that is possible.

In Act I the son of the true heir to the throne has just been told who he is and realizes the danger of incest. In Act II the other young man who is really the son of Phocas is told wrongly that he is the son of the murdered emperor, to save his friend. He also fears the danger of incest. In Act III the one who is the real son of the usurper is arrested and the daughter is threatened if she will not marry him. In Act IV the real son admits his identity and is not believed; but the tyrant at this time is in the position where he cannot kill either, because he knows one of them is his son and he does not know which. This is a source of very fine and very well worked-up pathos – of an inferior kind, I think; not the best that Corneille has ever produced, but very fine. In Act V the rather too clever stratagem, for which Corneille apologized, brings in a happy ending with an unhappy ending for the wicked party, such as we had in *Rodogune*.

Ironies and *double entendre* everywhere, and a new interest – or rather, not quite new since it had been used as early as *Cinna* – that of moves which are made by the characters engaging in the puzzle or the game of chess, and of which, at the moment, we do not see the purpose, and have the additional pleasure of trying to work it out. A work with an intellectual interest and, at the same time, a very great charge of suspense and excitement.

Once again after the excitement of these two plays we have a new waiting period where Corneille finds diversion, looks around and refreshes his powers of invention. The diversion is the machine play of *Andromède* which we know was all ready to be produced in 1647 though it was held back until 1660, after the Fronde was over and expensive productions could be contemplated again. I shall omit it here, and I think I can omit it without much inconvenience. Corneille himself said 'Cette pièce n'est que pour les yeux'.[4]

Don Sanche and *Nicomède*: swagger and 'admiration'

It is followed by a new pair of plays based on a new formula in a new pattern. He calls attention to the novelty in both, in very much the same terms, though he never admits that one is similar to the other, for one is not fully a tragedy. *Don Sanche d'Aragon* is, in our eyes, a tragicomedy. Corneille himself found a new name for it: 'comédie heroque'. If it owes anything to anybody it is to Rotrou, whose influence is present again in the other play of the couple, *Nicomède*. After his holiday with the machine play Corneille shows himself once again alive to the theatrical side of his drama. There is in this play a Spanish swagger, due perhaps to some of the sources, which is even greater than we find it in *Le Cid*. A new theme comes up, that of rank and *la race*, not in the racist sense of course, but in the sense of *le préjugé nobiliaire*, which appears here in all its glory. The hero is called Carlos; he is a mighty hero, he is a man of the people. He hides his birth but admits that he has no noble rank, thinking himself the son of a fisherman. He has been a great soldier and holds the kingdom of Seville in his hands as its deliverer.

Seigneur, pour mes parents je nomme mes exploits:
Ma valeur est ma race, et mon bras est mon père. (252–3)

A new thesis dead opposed to the beliefs of the reign. Did Corneille believe this? Or did he believe as he says elsewhere that generosity can only come from 'un sang généreux'; only the nobility can be noble? Is this perhaps a paradox made for the purpose of the play, to excite and puzzle? The answer is no clearer to the writer than to the reader. The hero, I said, refuses to call himself noble when a rumour makes it seem that he may be the long-lost Prince of the blood. He refuses that rank when it is offered to him, as long as it is dubious. Immediately afterwards the old fisherman discovers him, and Carlos with great *générosité* admits his sonship; accepts the old man with respect and, at the same time, with bitter regret for what he sees to be his *disgrâce*. But, of course, in the end the fisherman is not his father – he is the long-lost Prince. All is well and the *préjugé nobiliaire* is reconciled with the maxim that kind hearts are more than coronets. He stands up as much superior to the suitors of the queen whom he loves. He cannot aspire to her, not being noble. He cannot even sit down in the presence of the *Grands d'Espagne*, and the queen has to ennoble him. In the scene – which Victor Hugo remembered with gratitude in *Hernani* – to solve the problem of the marriage she must make, it is to him who cannot marry her that she entrusts her ring as a token: she will accept the candidate he approves. Whereupon he challenges each of the three to fight him in turn, and will recommend the one who can beat him. A duel that does not come off, but which reminds one rather of the *Trois Mousquetaires* than of anything else. The queen loves him secretly and we have a whole act, the third, of the casuistry of love in all the *précieux* complications that the century had discovered, in which she fights or comes to terms with her love. But he, on his side, loves or thinks he loves two women, both queens, the Queen of Castile and the Queen of Aragon, one of whom, of course, is going to turn out to be his sister. We have also a nobleman, don Alvar, who loves queen number two – Aragon – but is in line, and perhaps first in line, for number one – Castile – because of the 'tristes lois de l'honneur' which make it necessary for him to aspire to a throne if he can get it. We are here very much in the atmosphere which later produces the 'tragédie matrimoniale'.

Corneille wrote a long preface to this play, or rather an epistle to Christian Huyghens, M. de Zuylichem, discussing the nature of the thing he had produced, which, of course, as so often, he introduces as 'un poème d'une espèce nouvelle'. He will not call it a tragedy 'puisqu'on n'y voit naître aucun péril par qui nous puissions être portés à la pitié ou à la crainte'. If those are the hallmark of tragedy this cannot be a tragedy. It does, however, produce *de l'admiration* and this brings it into proximity with *Nicomède* for which, in fact, he makes the same point about *l'admiration* as being his new tragic emotion; and where, in fact, the Aristotelian emotions of pity and fear exist to a minimal degree.

When he writes *Nicomède* a year after, he repeats much of the matter of this epistle in the Preface and now seems to believe that here for the first time in tragedy, he is using this new emotion of *admiration*. We modern readers tend rather to think that it was not new in Corneille, and that he had always banked largely on this emotion and very much less, in all his tragedies, on pity and fear. In Horace, in Auguste, in Polyeucte (provided we approve of him), is not *admiration*, wonder, astonishment, the basis of all our emotion?

I would make three other points. First, that *générosité* as a motive is back. We have seen it in *Don Sanche*; we saw it, of course, as one of the great values in the Tetralogy: but it is caused now not by a moral crux, as it was, in fact, in *Cosroès*, the tragedy of Rotrou that Corneille used as the basis of the situation of *Nicomède*.[5] The only cause that Nicomède has to maintain is the independence of kings threatened by the expansion of Rome. But in this crux where he defends his father's rights in spite of his father, in spite of the danger of Rome, he is inflexible and, at the same time, sees no problem because he cannot conceive of any other attitude than the one he takes. And when he endures the consequences he makes no renunciation; he proves to his father that the dilemma he solves which his father set involves no real renunciation (1348 ff.). He shows mainly indignation. He wins in the end; it is interesting that he does not win by his own efforts, because Corneille has built for him, as he built for the two princes of *Rodogune* and he will make later for other people, such as Othon, a cage which makes it impossible for him to escape by his own efforts since he is inhibited by his moral principles. He is aggrieved in his rights as inheritor by his father and he will not resist or question his father. But by the magnetism of his own magnanimity he creates an ally in his half-brother Attale; he already has his betrothed who is a counterpart of himself, and their work makes for the triumphant close where the wicked are converted by example and a double ending with unhappiness for them is unnecessary.

The second point is Corneille's handling of history. He is rather more respectful here than he was in our last two plays, though, of course, the character and the plotting of Arsinoé, the wicked stepmother, is entirely his own invention. Plotting and wickedness which remind us of the queen in *Rodogune*, but are simpler. The respect is largely a show, because he omits to point out that, while he has changed 'les acheminements', which is what he said he felt free to change when he discussed the question in the foreword of *Rodogune*, he has also changed 'les effets que l'histoire nous donne'. History shows that Nicomedes, having triumphed over his father's wicked designs, did kill his father: our Nicomède refuses to. The subject gives the playwright a most impressive political theme in 'La politique des Romains' at this exact time: he shows that they were bound to absorb the whole of the Mediterranean world. 'Rome est en effet', says the ambassador, 'la maîtresse du monde.' And to describe that *politique* was, he says, 'mon principal but dans cette tragédie'. He brings in Hannibal, a great figure recently dead. He brings in the designs of Rome in the person of an ambassador, and the picture he draws, which is essentially accurate, historians say, has never been as ambitious in an earlier play. Later he will give us the same kind of historical picture, choosing always in the plays after the Fronde one or another period of the Roman Empire in its long decline and corruption. There are 'raisons d'Etat' connected with the position of the king, Prusias, too. We find that figure which we found as early as *Le Cid*, which we shall go on finding until the latest tragedy *Suréna* – the vassal too powerful for his master who, nevertheless, has performed enormous services for that master, who fears him.

It is a splendid play, the play I think I like the most of Corneille's after the Tetralogy. It moves more easily, more powerfully, more elegantly than any other play before or perhaps since. It is a model of construction; I think I would say the model of classical tragedy if any one play had to be named in that role. It uses conspiracy, plotting, cleverly, with complexity but not undue complexity. It has a beautiful denouement with gradation and surprise, two *péripéties* and real emotion, communicative as in *Cinna*, caused by *générosité*. It contains the best writing of any of the plays so far. The speeches are shorter; the dialogue is fast, flashing, violent but elegant and witty, especially when Nicomède appears. Corneille is right back on form; and if we are speaking of form only, or mainly, in distinction from content, in better form than he would ever appear again or has ever appeared.

Unfortunately this is not the end of our period. We have one more play; and in it Corneille turns his back on his achievement and falls flat on his face.

Pertharite: goodbye to *gloire*

Pertharite, the next play, was a worse failure than *Théodore*; Corneille's worst failure, after which in his Preface he simply spoke of saying goodbye to the theatre. He had made a new change of direction, the most violent he had yet made. Very little, in fact, as he discovered, separates the production of *admiration* by surprise and the production of shock and disapproval. *Pertharite* does not deserve the failure it incurred, in my opinion. I would not say it had the brilliance of *Nicomède*. It is certain that it is broken-backed, as *Horace* and *Cinna* had been, by changing the situation radically in the middle of the play; but it is a most intelligent play. The last problem treated in it is the question, what do you do if a king whom you have dethroned survives his defeat? And the answer, in case the reader does not think of it at once, is that unless you kill him and all his kin, you might as well give him back the throne which you have taken from him; because, unless he has the tact like Charles II to remove himself, there is no third way. As everyone knows, the play begins with the situation, complete in all its parts, which Racine took over for *Andromaque*. But there is another thing also, which I want to refer to here; I have written of it before[6] and I must not make too much of it now. There is a complete show-up, if not a send-up, of the values of, perhaps not *la générosité* but *le héros glorieux*. *Générosité* survives: Pertharite is *généreux* but in a new way. Heroism is shown, though in other ways. But the Queen, the model of Andromaque, who begins by being, though rather self-assertive, rather sure of herself – a copybook of all that a character like Cornélie had stood for – suddenly appears in a new light; it will perhaps be remembered that she had created the kind of shock that Corneille counted on by answering the demand of the tyrant, Grimoald, that she should marry him, with the challenge that she would marry him only if Grimoald killed her son whom he had been threatening, and thereby incurred hatred. A bluff; she is counting on his better nature and, if one re-reads the play one then discovers that she shows more signs of horror and suffering herself than a first or even a second reading may lead one to think. But she is self-assertive, she is sure of her values, which are the Baroque values (if you like the word), and then is herself shocked to the marrow by the return of her fugitive husband who was not killed on the battlefield after all – her husband who turns to the king and says that he finds he cannot resist any further, he can get no support, so the usurper may have the crown but he wants his wife back: 'Garde mon diadème . . .; Laisse-moi racheter Rodélinde à ce prix.'[7] In the version of 1653, later softened down, his wife refuses to recognize him and says that he must be an impostor, since he has not the language of a true king. Before the end, he forces us to see that he is the truly human and, in a way, truly heroic figure; realistic, unwilling to sacrifice for unreal ends, ready, however, to make a total sacrifice of his own life (1420–84), so that she may marry the usurper and keep the crown, which to her has been the highest duty of a royal figure. This melts her, and they are reconciled; but not before she has shown up as a superannuated model of a heroism which Corneille has given up. This, I suppose, is what made the play fail; the public was not ready for it. This was 'l'évenément extraordinaire qui me l'avait fait choisir', says Corneille (though in fact his memory had failed him: he had invented the act of the king, which is not in any of his sources). But, there you are; carry originality, the art of paradox, the production of *admiration*, too far and it will shock and it will cause your failure. Corneille was to do it again later on; this, I think, is the key to *Sertorius* and *Othon*, which belong to a later part of this study.

IV

Corneille Returns

It is impossible to say whether, during the 'holiday' of seven years (1652–59) that he took from his playwright's career, Corneille was meditating and maturing in his mind the new type of tragedy that was about to appear.

The interval was filled by the production of several thousand pieces of devotional verse – *L'Imitation de Jésus-Christ*, a translation of à Kempis (begun even before *Pertharite*), ably and elegantly done, if with no conspicuous sign of personal commitment. It was filled also, towards the end, with preparations for the three-volume quarto edition of his *Théâtre complet* (1660), a 'retrospective' display of his achievement, carefully – but sometimes regrettably – edited and corrected in accordance with the language and taste of the second half of the century, and accompanied or prefaced with three *Discours* on the drama which the preface (1654) to the last instalment of his *Imitation* shows to have been meditated long in advance.

***Les Discours*: coming to terms with Aristotle**

To accompany the great edition Corneille wrote what he must have seen as the authoritative statement of the aims and principles of the tragic genre he had created. The only competitor was the Abbé d'Aubignac's *Pratique du Théâtre*, compiled during the great moments of the early forties, but held back until 1657 after Richelieu had died and financial support disappeared. It made no great sensation, and Corneille affects to ignore it, still accompanied as he is by all the glory of the never-equalled Tetralogy and a string of later plays, less successful but still well received.

His 'doctrine', as it appears in the *Discours* and the *Examens* which accompany each play in the 1660 volume, has been too fully treated by my friend H.T. Barnwell[1] for there to be any necessity to attempt the task again; I shall simply touch on points of interest and speak of the merits I see in this important work.

It is right to see his *Discours* as polemic, apologetic and explanatory of his own achievement – but retrospectively, alas: there are no clues here that we can use for puzzling features of the plays yet to come after

1660. It is at the same time a lucid, painstaking and able exposition of Aristotle's *Poetics* – of that work alone among the few critical treatises of antiquity, but with abundant evidence of the study of numerous commentators (although he quotes only two, Castelvetro and Heinsius, of the ten listed as required reading in d'Aubignac's *Pratique du théâtre*.[2] He apologizes cheerfully that he could not bring himself to read more deeply, 'et je m'assure que beaucoup de mes lecteurs me pardonneront aisément cette paresse'! He has found ideas which were useful to him in the *Poetics*, though the work enshrines the two least helpful doctrines of the age, both creations of bigotry, misconception, and even mistranslation:[3] that of catharsis, believed to require a directly moral aim in art, and that of vraisemblance, the parent of the Unities and all notions of stage illusion. The philosopher's name is quoted in the first sentence of the first *Discours*, and there is hardly a page where his text is not reproduced, with deep deference, by Corneille to save his ideal of the striking, unexpected ending, but a deference which does not exclude the possibility of irony or independence:

> Cependant . . . il est aisé de nous accommoder avec Aristote. Nous n'avons qu'à dire que . . . (B 34)

He writes with studied moderation:

> J'écris sans ambition and sans esprit de contestation . . . Je tâche de suivre toujours le sentiment d'Aristote . . .; et comme peut-être je l'entends à ma mode, je ne suis point jaloux qu'un autre l'entende à la sienne . . . J'ai pris pour m'expliquer, un style simple . . . (27)

His first *Discours* is entitled *de l'utilité et des parties du Poème dramatique*. The first paragraph contains a resolute right-and-left against his old adversaries: 'Bien que, selon Aristote, le seul but de la poésie dramatique soit de plaire aux spectateurs' – and Richelieu's group had always insisted on the primary importance of the moral aim of art; and, second, 'on en est venu jusqu'à établir une maxime très fausse, qu'*il faut que le sujet d'une tragédie soit vraisemblable*, appliquant ainsi aux conditions du sujet [the story itself] la moitié de ce qu'il a dit de la manière de la traiter' (for he had spoken of 'le vraisembable *ou le nécessaire*') (B 1–2).

He returns to *la vraisemblance*, to insist on his belief (which we already know) that, while an invented *sujet* should of course be *vraisemblable*, the kind the tragic poet wants –

> les grands sujets qui remuent fortement les passions, et en opposent l'impétuosité aux lois du devoir ou aux tendresses du sang, doivent toujours aller au-delà du vraisemblable

and need the authority of history or myth to convince:

> il n'est past vraisemblable que Médée tue ses enfants, que Clytemnestre assassine son mari, qu'Oreste poignarde sa mère; mais l'histoire le dit, et la représentation de ces grands crimes ne trouve point d'incrédules'. (B 2)

At the same time, he takes care to adopt a moderate, eirenic and reasonable attitude: 'Il est constant qu'il y a des préceptes, puisqu'il y a un art . . .' (*un art* being for him a difficult pursuit of which one had to know the secrets: and it would be foolish to neglect the short cuts already discovered):

> mais il n'est pas constant quels ils sont . . . Il faut donc savoir quelles sont ces règles; mais notre malheur est qu'Aristote et Horace après lui en ont écrit assez obscurément pour avoir besoin d'interprètes, et que ceux qui leur en ont voulu servir jusques ici ne les ont souvent expliqués qu'en grammairiens ou en philosophes. Comme ils avaient plus d'étude et de spéculation que d'expérience du théâtre, leur lecture nous peut rendre plus doctes, mais non pas nous donner beaucoup de lumières fort sûres pour y réussir.
>
> Je hasarderai quelque chose sur trente ans de travail pour la scène, et en dirai mes pensées tout simplement, sans esprit de contestation qui m'engage à les soutenir, et sans prétendre que personne renonce en ma faveur à celles qu'il en aura conçues. (B 3)

Returning to 'l'utilité', he concedes that, while not precisely required, it cannot be neglected; of the four ways he proposes of introducing it the most interesting (and to us recommendable) is 'la naïve peinture des vices et des vertus, qui ne manque jamais à faire son effet' (B 5). The fourth is of course the famous catharsis, *la purgation des passions*, of which more will be heard anon.

He comes to Aristotle's 'parts of quantity' (the constituent parts of drama: plot, or action, character, sentiment, etc.) and I shall quote his definitions of the tragic 'action' as distinguished from the comic:

> Sa dignité demande quelque grand intérêt d'Etat, ou quelque passion plus noble et plus mâle que l'amour, telles que sont l'ambition ou la vengeance, . . . Il est à propos d'y mêler

> l'amour, parce qu'il a toujours beaucoup d'agrément, et peut servir de fondement à ces intérêts, et à ces autres passions dont je parle; mais il faut qu'il se contente du second rang dans le poème. (B 8)

Under 'character' he has trouble with Aristotle's demand that 'les mœurs' should be 'bonnes' (B 14); he comes up with a striking formula which expresses well his own idea of the 'héros en mal' that he had been using from *Rodogune* to *Héraclius*:

> S'il m'est permis de dire mes conjectures sur ce qu'Aristote nous demande par là, je crois que c'est le caractère brillant et élevé d'une habitude vertueuse ou criminelle . . . Cléopâtre, dans *Rodogune*, est très méchante, il n'y a point de parricide qui lui fasse horreur, pourvu qu'il la puisse conserver sur un trône qu'elle préfère à toutes choses, tant son attachement à la domination est violent; mais tous ses crimes sont accompagnés d'une grandeur d'âme qui a quelque chose de si haut, qu'en même temps qu'on déteste ses actions, on admire la source dont elles partent. (ibid.)

Skipping a textual corruption in the *Poetics* (B 15) which leaves Corneille helpless, we come to 'les parties de quantité', the sections into which a Greek tragedy can be divided, 'qui sont le prologue, l'épisode, l'exode et le choeur' (B 20); Corneille equates them with the exposition, the acts in the middle, and the denouement. Largely from his own experience, he draws up a code of practice for the shapely and compact play, I almost said *la pièce bien faite*. There are some memorable formulas here.

> Je voudrais donc que le premier acte contînt le fondement de toutes les actions, et fermât la porte à tout ce qu'on voudrait introduire d'ailleurs dans le reste du poème. (B 22)

For Act V: 'Il faut, s'il se peut, lui réserver toute la catastrophe, et même la reculer vers la fin' (B 26), to keep the audience on the edge of its seats waiting for it.

At the end,

> Le spectateur doit être si bien instruit des sentiments de tous ceux qui y ont eu quelque part, qu'il sorte l'esprit en repos, et ne soit plus en doute de rien. (B 10)

Corneille had not always been faithful to this exacting and rather mechanical code, and will not always be in future; but it is his ideal, constructed by him from the *Poetics*.

The second *Discours*, 'de la Tragédie et des moyens de la traiter selon le vraisemblable ou le nécessaire', begins with the famous purgation of the passions through pity and fear, which Corneille tries to expound, but without success – for it has never been successfully explained until the mid-nineteenth century: it refers, as we know now, to a beneficial release of emotional tension. He quotes Aristotle to the effect that '*nous avons pitié . . . de ceux que nous voyons souffrir un malheur qu'ils ne méritent pas, et nous craignons qu'il ne nous en arrive un pareil, quand nous le voyons souffrir à nos semblables*' (B 28) and tries to follow his thought:

> La pitie d'un malheur où nous voyons tomber nos semblables nous porte à la crainte d'un pareil pour nous; cette crainte, au désir de l'éviter; et ce désir, à purger, modérer, rectifier, et même déraciner en nous la passion qui plonge à nos yeux dans ce malheur les personnes que nous plaignons, par cette raison commune, mais naturelle et indubitable, que pour éviter l'effet il faut retrancher la cause. (B 29)

but he remains perplexed and produces a frank and disarming confession:

> J'avoue donc avec franchise que je n'entends point l'application de cet exemple.
>
> J'avouerai plus. Si la purgation des passions se fait dans la tragédie, je tiens qu'elle se doit faire de la manière que je l'explique; mais je doute si elle s'y fait jamais, et dans celles-là même qui ont les conditions que demande Aristote. Elles se rencontrent dans *le Cid*, et en ont causé le grand succès. Rodrigue et Chimène y ont cette probité sujette aux passions, et ces passions font leur malheur, . . . leur malheur fait pitié, . . . Cette pitié nous doit donner une crainte de tomber dans un pareil malheur, et purger en nous ce trop d'amour qui cause leur infortune et nous les fait plaindre; mais je ne sais si elle nous la donne, ni si elle le purge, et j'ai bien peur que le raisonnement d'Aristote sur ce point ne soit qu'une belle idée qui n'ait jamais son effet dans la vérité. (B 32)

A flat contradiction then, politely wrapped up.

But Corneille advances into 'les moyens d'exciter cette pitié' (37). The action (assumed to involve murder) must be 'entre proches', not between enemies or parties indifferent to each other. Aristotle debates the patterns in which it can take place – does the doer know? will he desist? (B 39) – and Corneille, though politely, is in disagreement with the philosopher's preference. That the victim should not be known is to Corneille inadmissible; the case produces too little emotion, and, even if the killing and recognition take place, there is too little time left for emotion. He relies on his own dramatic experience to contradict Aristotle:

> . . . Lorsqu'on agit à visage découvert, et qu'on sait à qui on en veut, le combat des passions . . . occupe la meilleure partie du poème, et de là naissent les grandes et fortes émotions . . .
>
> (See the whole passage, quoted p. 52)

Incognitos spoil great tragedy and 'le goût de notre siècle' is against that of the Greeks (B 43).

Several pages debating what changes are allowed or required, to make such subjects fit for the public to see, bring him back for the last time to vraisemblance. His lawyer's eye has discovered an escape in the text he is expounding:

> [Aristote] nous apprend que *le poète n'est pas obligé de traiter les choses comme elles se sont passées, mais comme elles ont pu ou dû se passer, selon le vraisemblable ou le nécessaire*. Il répète souvent ces derniers mots, et ne les explique jamais. Je tâcherai d'y suppleér au moins mal qu'il me sera possible. (B 49)

What then is this *nécessaire*, which is given to the playwright as an alternative and never explained by him or any commentator? (and why does this word sometimes appear before the other?). We cannot help admiring the ingenuity with which he brings out his discovery – totally unjustified I am afraid: the literal translation is 'What is possible according to likelihood or necessity', i.e. 'What is likely, or bound, to happen'. But no, in the light of these scandalous killings which the *Poetics* prefers to see corrected, or of a simple improbability caused by the Unities, 'le nécessaire . . . n'est autre chose que *le besoin du poète pour arriver à son but ou pour y faire arriver ses acteurs*' (B 59). How simple! – whatever the playwright feels he cannot avoid, he has the philosopher's permission to do.

Corneille concludes (with reference to the poet's right to alter his stories:

> . . . *Dabiturque licentia sumpta pudenter*.
>
> Servons-nous-en donc avec retenue, mais sans scrupule, et s'il se peut, ne nous en servons point du tout. Il vaut mieux n'avoir point besoin de grâce que d'en recevoir. (B 61)

This endpiece gives the tone to the whole third *Discours* (*des trois unités, d'action, de jour, et de lieu*). He accepts these constraints with a good grace, provided they can be *apprivoisées*.

On the first Unity he has little remarkable to say. He makes it consist 'dans la comédie, en l'unité d'intrique [sic] ou d'obstacle aux desseins des principaux acteurs, et en l'unité de péril dans la tragédie' (B 62). He proposes rules for a 'liaison des scènes' (which 'n'est qu'un ornement et non pas une règle' [64]). In denouements two things are to be avoided, 'le simple changement de volonté, et la machine [*deus ex machina*]' (B 67 f). He discusses the number of acts and scenes, and the management of exits and entrances (B 69 f.) and writes an interesting note on the need for stage directions (B 70 f.).

Unity of Time he accepts without protest (even misquoting the clause which all had misquoted before him, 'que la tragédie *doit* renfermer la durée de son action . . .' (71) where the *Poetics* are content to say that 'Tragedy endeavours to keep as far as possible within . . .' (Bywater, 49ª13). Not without qualifications however:

> Pour moi, je trouve qu'il y a des sujets si malaisés à renfermer en si peu de temps, que non seulement je leur accorderais les vingt-quatre heures entières, mais je me servirais même de la licence que donne ce philosophe de les excéder un peu, et les pousserais sans scrupule jusqu'à trente. Nous avons une maxime en droit qu'il faut élargir la faveur, et restreindre les rigueurs, *odia restingenda, favores ampliandi*, et je trouve qu'un auteur est assez gêné par cette contrainte, qui a forcé quelques-uns de nos anciens d'aller jusqu'à l'impossible.
>
> (B 71–2)

And he cites *The Suppliants* and *Agamemnon*. But he goes on to approve the reasoning (not the text of the *Poetics*, but the argument drawn from *vraisemblance*) behind the rule, concluding nevertheless:

> La représentation dure deux heures, et ressemblerait parfaitement, si l'action qu'elle représente n'en demandait pas davantage pour sa réalité. Ainsi ne nous arrêtons point ni aux douze, ni aux vingt-quatre heures; mais resserrons l'action du poème dans la moindre durée qu'il nous sera possible, afin que sa représentation ressemble mieux et soit plus parfaite. Ne donnons, s'il se peut, à l'une [l'action] que les deux heures que l'autre [la représentation] remplit . . . Si nous ne pouvons la renfermer dans ces deux heures, prenons-en quatre, six, dix,

> mais ne passons pas de beaucoup les vingt-quatre, de peur de tomber dans le déréglement . . .
>
> Surtout je voudrais laisser cette durée à l'imagination des auditeurs, et ne déterminer jamais le temps qu'elle emporte . . . (B 72 f.).

The rest of the time supposed to elapse must pass in the intervals; and the last act must be allowed to contain more than the clock allows (for the public must not be kept waiting for the sake of *vraisemblance* to find out what happens) (B 73 f.).

Unity of Place causes trouble because women characters commonly need a private room each (B 76), and royalties cannot be made to speak in the market-place (B 77). Corneille would therefore grant 'très volontiers que ce qu'on ferait passer en une seule ville aurait l'unité de lieu. Ce n'est pas que je voulusse que le théâtre représentât cette ville toute entière, cela serait un peu trop vaste, mais seulement deux ou trois lieux particuliers enfermés dans l'enclos de ses murailles' (ibid.). Unfortunately he never tells us how he would have staged this – two compartments, one always curtained off? He remembers, and recalls, the large number of locations for which he will apologize in the *Examen* of *Le Cid*. But the difficulty can be smoothed over:

> Je voudrais qu'on fît deux choses: l'une, que jamais on ne changeât dans le même acte, mais seulement de l'une à l'autre . . . l'autre, que ces deux lieux n'eussent point besoin de diverses décorations, et qu'aucun des deux ne fût jamais nommé . . . Cela aiderait à tromper l'auditeur, qui ne voyant rien qui lui marquât la diversité des lieux, ne s'en apercevrait pas, à moins d'une réflexion malicieuse et critique, dont il y en a peu qui soient capables, la plupart s'attachant avec chaleur à l'action qu'ils voient représenter. (ibid.)

This happens constantly in Corneille's mature plays; in *Nicomède* the king actually says 'Rendons-lui [à Laonice] donc visite' (741) and the next act is in her quarters. But if no change may be made within an act, there is also the question of deadly secret discussions where walls may have ears.

> Les jurisconsultes admettent des fictions de droit; et je voudrais, à leur exemple, introduire des fictions de théâtre, pour établir un lieu théâtral qui ne serait ni l'appartement de Cléopâtre, ni celui de Rodogune dans la pièce qui porte ce titre . . . mais une salle sur laquelle ouvrent ces divers appartements, à qui j'attribuerais

> deux privilèges: l'un, que chacun de ceux qui y parleraient fût présumé y parler avec le même secret que s'il était dans sa chambre; [and the other, that *la bienséance* should never force characters to leave the stage to visit superior personages].
>
> (B 78 f.)

He winds up with great effect, in the character of the old warrior who has learnt wisdom, moderation and indulgence:

> Beaucoup de mes pièces en manqueront [manqueront d'unité de lieu] si l'on ne veut point admettre cette modération, dont je me contenterai toujours à l'avenir, quand je ne pourrai satisfaire à la dernière rigueur de la règle. Je n'ai pu y en réduire que trois: *Horace*, *Polyeucte* et *Pompée*. Si je me donne trop d'indulgence dans les autres, j'en aurai encore davantage pour ceux dont je verrai réussir les ouvrages sur la scène avec quelque apparence de régularité. Il est facile aux spéculatifs d'être sévères; mais s'ils voulaient donner dix ou douze poèmes de cette nature au public, ils élargiraient peut-être les règles encore plus que je ne fais, sitôt qu'ils auraient reconnu par l'expérience quelle contrainte apporte leur exactitude, et combien de belles choses elle bannit de notre théâtre. Quoi qu'il en soit, voilà mes opinions, ou si vous voulez, mes hérésies touchant les principaux points de l'art; et je ne sais point mieux accorder les règles anciennes avec les agréments modernes. Je ne doute point qu'il ne soit aisé d'en trouver de meilleurs moyens, et je serai tout prêt de les suivre lorsqu'on les aura mis en pratique aussi heureusement qu'on y a vu les miens.
>
> (B 79)

But the effect may change if we read his comment to his friend the Abbé de Pure:

> Je suis à la fin d'un travail fort pénible sur une matière fort delicate . . . J'y ai fait quelques explications nouvelles d'Aristote, et avancé quelques propositions et quelques maximes inconnues à nos Anciens. J'y réfute celles sur lesquelles l'Académie a fondé la condamnation du Cid, et ne suis pas d'accord avec M. d'Aubignac de tout le bien même qu'il a dit de moi . . .
> . . . Vous n'y trouverez pas grande élocution, ni grande doctrine; mais avec tout cela, j'avoue que ces trois préfaces m'ont plus coûté que n'auraient fait trois pièces de théâtre . . .Bien que je contredise quelquefois M. d'Aubignac et

> messieurs de l'Académie, je ne les nomme jamais, et ne parle non plus d'eux que s'ils n'avaient point parlé de moi.[4]

It worked. One has only to sense the rage with which, in a fourth *Dissertation* following attacks on Corneille's last three plays, d'Aubignac expostulates that a critic need not be a successful playwright, and that his plays anyhow had not been *that* bad.[5]

Œdipe: Corneille versus Sophocles

Almost alone in the seventeenth century,[6] Corneille – not Racine – measured himself against Sophocles. Sophocles was the most highly admired of Greek playwrights, and his *Oedipus Rex* was known to have been particularly admired by Aristotle – but the hypocrisy and emptiness of this kind of conventional praise has been shown up by Noémi Hepp in relation to Homer.[7]

The play Corneille wrote in 1659 should not be made to provide too much evidence of his ideas on tragedy, since according to his own account it was coaxed out of him by Foucquet's patronage, and the choice of subject was not his own. Whether or not the naïve surprise expressed in the *Au Lecteur* and *Examen* is genuine or over-played, at finding the subject of *Œdipe* so far from helpful to the adapter, we do not know; *Oedipus Rex* was known to be Aristotle's favourite in Greek drama, and was praised universally as 'le chef-d'œuvre de l'antiquité', but it had been noticeably avoided by imitators in the seventeenth century. Corneille of course left his trademark. The play is relatively short (as all Greek plays are) and the gap has been filled with a newly invented subject (somewhat as we have seen in *Cinna*) and this subject, after an obligatory reference to the plague raging in Thebes, leads on to quite new material, of a much more familiar, political cast. A female character has been invented here also – Dircé, the one surviving offspring of Laïus and Jocaste besides the son, believed dead; and she provides a pretty constitutional problem within the traditional mythical subject; for Dircé is the legitimate heiress (always supposing the Greek states behaved like modern European ones in the matter of succession) who has been defrauded of her rights by the gratitude of the people, who gave the crown to Œdipe in reward for his delivery of the city from the ravages of the Sphinx – a thing the people had no right to do according to Dircé:

S'il eût eu pour son Roi quelque ombre d'amitié,
Si mon sexe ou mon âge eût ému sa pitié,
Il n'aurait jamais eu cette lâche faiblesse,
De livrer en vos mains l'Etat et sa princesse, (439 ff.)

Viewed as an *épisode* in the treatment of the myth, this is strictly an irrelevance – unless perhaps introduced to blacken slightly the character of Œdipe, who as tragic hero must not be faultless. The grievance is presented as genuine – a slight that must have wounded the girl of five who was passed over with her own mother's acquiescence, but it seems to have ruffled relations little in more recent years. The play scarcely becomes a 'matrimonial tragedy' because of it, since Dircé does not desire to marry Thésée, the neighbouring King of Athens, for political reasons, though Œdipe has political reasons for wishing to stop her; what Dircé wants is to marry the man she loves and who loves her. The motive makes the engrafted episode a piece of typical *tragédie galante* such as Thomas Corneille and Quinault were writing; for Thésée (whom Racine was to paint eighteen years later as the reformed rake who married Phèdre) takes no more account of political considerations or obligations than does Dircé; in the eyes of both, the base populace, 'ces petites âmes' (687), matter nothing and are owed nothing by their rulers, who are there by divine ordinance:

Ce n'est pas au peuple à se faire justice:
L'ordre que tient le ciel à lui choisir des rois
Ne lui permet jamais d'examiner son choix . . . (1634 ff.)

There is indeed an obligation to give one's life for the people if a god demands it; but this is dictated by a cold sense of *gloire* and springs from no love or patriotism.

When Thésée makes the claim, which has so much interested our politically minded critics of Corneille, that he must, or may, be the long-lost heir of Laïus, it is a characteristic piece of bluff (like those of Sabine or Rodélinde), made in complete insincerity with the generous motive of saving Dircé from giving her life in response to the demand of Laïus' shade for 'le sang de *sa* race' (606). Thésée says in effect 'Can anyone prove that I am not?', and all remember that he had had difficulty in making good his claim to be the son of Aegeus (Egée – yes, the Egée of *Médée*; how inopportunely these French classical allusions come in!). Dircé does not seem to believe him (1258 ff.), but appreciates his motive, as her tender play on the words *frère* and *amant* shows. Jocaste does not believe him either; she only half accepts that his love for Dircé, if he is her brother, would attest incestuous tendencies; but to fulfil the specification he must also have killed his father (1137 ff.). This imputation draws from the young man the well-known repudiation of all belief in an overruling fate:

Quoi? la nécessité des vertus et des vices
D'un astre impérieux doit suivre les caprices,
Et Delphes, malgré nous, conduit nos actions
Au plus bizarre effet de ses prédictions?
L'âme est donc toute esclave; une loi souveraine
Vers le bien ou le mal incessamment l'entraîne,
Et nous ne recevons ni crainte ni désir
De cette liberté qui n'a rien à choisir,
Attachés sans relâche à cet ordre sublime,
Vertueux sans mérite, et vicieux sans crime.
. . .
D'un tel aveuglement daignez me dispenser.
Le ciel, juste à punir, juste à récompenser,
Pour rendre aux actions leur peine ou leur salaire,
Doit nous offrir son aide, et puis nous laisser faire.

(1149 ff.)

(Thésée is free to scoff at the very data of the tragedy; Œdipe is not.)

The clouds close in (not before Act III Scene 4), in time to close the debates on Thésée's claim and Œdipe's tyranny: though we do have the un-Sophoclean sight of the putative son challenging the putative murderer to a duel (1487 ff. – an anachronism which was 'un crime de théâtre', in the eyes of the author of the *Examen* of *Horace*). Corneille takes some pride in having smoothed away *invraisemblances* and undue prolixity in oracular utterances (see *Au Lecteur*); as author of *Héraclius* he must have felt well qualified to revise the engineering of these effects. Indeed, he seems to have seen the *Oedipus* as no more than an exercise in detective procedures and a study of the sorry injustice of the dealings of gods with men.

Œdipe is the last of the broken-backed actions: Unity of Action for Corneille as we know should be secured by the Unity of Peril, but this unity has been broken by the Dircé episode, which cannot be said to have endangered the hero, nor led him into a greater peril.

At last comes the confrontation of the reluctant witnesses, and the realization of the ghastly truth (only five short scenes from the end – the final peripety cannot come too late, according to Corneille). There is a touching last scene (V. 5) between the incestuous pair, before

Jocaste takes her life on learning the complete revelation. Œdipe, with iron self-control, leaves the stage (where Corneille will not allow him to reappear with his eyes torn out), and deceives his guard into letting him act. He has maintained throughout that

> Mon souvenir n'est plein que d'exploits généreux,
> Cependant je me trouve inceste et parricide,
> Sans avoir fait un pas que sur les pas d'Alcide.
> . . .
> Hélas! qu'il est bien vrai qu'en vain on s'imagine
> Dérober notre vie à ce qu'il [le Ciel] nous destine!
> . . .
> Mais si les Dieux m'ont fait la vie abominable,
> Ils m'en font par pitié la sortie honorable,
> Puisque enfin leur faveur mêlée à leur courroux
> Me condamne à mourir pour le salut de tous,
> Et qu'en ce même temps qu'il faudrait que ma vie
> Des crimes qu'ils m'ont faits traînât l'ignominie,
> L'éclat de ces vertus que je ne tiens pas d'eux
> Reçoit pour récompense un trépas glorieux. (1820 ff.)

– and we must no doubt see that in thus fulfilling the oracle by shedding his blood, but remaining at the same time a living reproach (for he does not die, yet) against divine injustice (cf. 1991 ff.), he has made his dignified protest and retains the respect of all witnesses.

> Mais quand ce coup tombé vient d'épuiser le sort
> Jusqu'à n'en pouvoir craindre un plus barbare effort,
> Ce trouble se dissipe, et cette âme innocente,
> Qui brave impunément la fortune impuissante,
> Regarde avec dédain ce qu'elle a combattu,
> Et se rend tout entière à toute sa vertu. (1891 ff.)

And Corneille has converted Sophocles to his view of life.

La Toison d'or

La Toison d'or, which followed *Oedipe*, was another commissioned piece, and like *Andromède* a machine-play. It has nothing at all to deserve the title 'tragedy', except presumably the divine or royal status of the characters. Corneille brings in the figure of Hypsipyle, who had entertained Jason and his Argonauts on her island of Lemnos, and received Jason's promise of marriage. From Act II the action hinges on the rivalry of Hypsipyle and Médée, daughter of the King of Colchos, where Jason has come to carry off the Fleece – he needs the help of Médée's magic powers to do so; each queen knows Jason has broken faith, but is still in love with him. This most un-Cornelian attitude is to be excused in Médeé by the wiles (but not the magic) of Junon, who favours Jason. The lavish décor includes natural scenes, a garden, a palace, with aerial combats and *changements à vue* – but no spectacle derived from the magic events in the story which, one would think, had made Corneille choose it: no fire-breathing bulls, no warriors sprung from serpents' teeth. The denouement is muddled and seems to be hastily written; it comes as a great surprise to all concerned, and no doubt to the audience. After Jason has subdued the bulls and made the warriors kill one another (but by whose help and advice? we are not told), Médée, whom we thought to be unrelenting, lays the Fleece on the dragon, mounts, and takes off in the air towards the Argo, explaining that

> Du pays et du sang l'amour rompt les liens,
> Et les dieux de Jason sont plus forts que les miens. (2110 f.)

In an elaborate theophany – with no fewer that three upper stages in the theatre employed as the palaces or 'ciels' of three deities (all open and visible at the same time) – Jupiter settles the future of Médée's father, hints at her future abandonment by Jason (the subject of Corneille's old tragedy *Médée*), and adds that a son of Jason will found 'l'empire des Mèdes'.

The play is interesting only as showing Corneille's heroines forsaking all the standards of conduct that distinguish his tragedies – no doubt because he saw such sentiments as inescapable in his subject, and not unbecoming in a *machine*.

V

Tragedy Without Heroes: the matrimonial group

Free to please himself after the commissioned play *Œdipe* (another success which characteristically he refuses to follow up) Corneille enters into a decidedly changed atmosphere, that of the 'Matrimonial Group' of tragedies. In the world he has lately been creating, the path to power is in Court intrigue, not in the field, and heroism means nothing more than the pursuit of political aims with single-minded pertinacity by alliances and intrigues. Crowns are not to be won by fighting: few heroes now are victorious fighters: not even Nicomède, who has been one, but who owes his triumph to his supporters; Carlos (*Don Sanche*) does not win his crown eventually by victories; Sertorius and his enemy Pompée, eventually master of the situation, owe only their present precarious status to their military prowess. It is as if Corneille had seen the heroes of the Fronde from too near – *maior e longinquo reverentia*, as Racine was to point out. No, crowns are won by treaties, and treaties are usually sealed by marriages. *L'amour* and *la politique* still remain the two poles of Cornelian tragedy – the second term meaning all the problems of a statesman from foreign policy to 'intrigues de cabinet', including all the cares and ambitions concerning power in a state, or the power of a state among other states, the first term being the inescapable theme of the period (and most other modern periods), but turning up in this context as the enemy to *la raison d'Etat*. Heroism, the painful putting aside of a good, but a good of an inferior order, in favour of what the hero sees as a supreme value, would seem then to have a privileged field here.

But it is not so. Only in two of the seven 'matrimonial' plays is love heroically suppressed (*Sophonisbe*, *Pulchérie*); two others call far more attention to the painful struggle and the suffering of the victors, *Agésilas* and *Tite et Bérénice*. The heroes of the two tragedies we shall consider first are simply failures, who have set themselves tasks that prove too hard, and indeed of Sertorius Stegmann says very justly that 'Corneille ne cherche plus à nous faire admirer un héros . . . il veut nous émouvoir au spectacle d'un cœur déchiré pour qui le sacrifice est trop lourd'.[1] Surprisingly, his case was never condemned or even noticed by critics of the seventeenth or eighteenth century, but he has shocked one modern scholar, Professor P. Butler, who finds, with some grounds for his verdict, that 'dans un théâtre qui est celui de l'exaltation héroïque et de la volonté triomphante, l'échec du héros est, en soi, comique'.[2]

The two tragedies are linked by the fact that their Roman heroes are both in a sense great – the one, Sertorius, by his past exploits in the civil war, the other, Othon, only, it is true, by his ambitions for the future. *Sertorius* and *Othon* do not follow one another consecutively: the same pattern seems to continue that we have already noticed – a marked change of direction in the second of the group (*Sophonisbe*) followed by and cancelled by a change of manner which makes the third, *Othon*, almost a mirror image of the first, *Sertorius*, forming a cluster where the middle contrasts sharply with the pair surrounding it. *Sophonisbe*, the middle piece (1663), returns, at least in appearance, to the heroic theme of patriotism and the sacrifice of love.

The only possible appeal against Butler's condemnation of *Sertorius* is to ask if 'l'exaltation héroïque' and 'la volonté triomphante' are really characteristic of Cornelian tragedy, and not simply of a few outstanding figures (Rodrigue, Horace in Act II only, Auguste in Act V of *Cinna*, and Polyeucte) which have dazzled the public, and admittedly were meant to dazzle. I have tried to show *Pertharite* as the farewell appearance of the hero/heroine who is *généreux* and *glorieux*.

Sertorius: *quand un Romain soupire*

It is time to examine *Sertorius* more closely. I hope no reader will complain that I have given this play and *Othon*, which almost immediately follows it, too much space. They are interesting in themselves; they profoundly affect the total view we must take of Corneille; and they must be little known and have received little critical attention. The first act brings forward three politic lovers of the type described. The first to appear, the lieutenant Perpenna, is already almost committed to assassinating his commander Sertorius; but he also loves Sertorius's ally Viriate, queen of Nertobriga (marriage with whom would be advantageous), and relies on his general's support (if the assassination is called off!) to obtain her hand.

Sertorius himself is weighing the political advantages of a possible match with Pompée's divorced wife Aristie, who burns to escape the slight her husband was forced to lay on her, and who could bring over powerful Roman friends; or alternatively of a match with Viriate. To Perpenna he admits his attachment to the last-named, but shamefacedly because of his advanced age:

A mon âge il sied si mal d'aimer
Que je le cache même à qui m'a su charmer.
Mais tel que je puis être, on m'aime, ou pour mieux dire,
La reine Viriate à mon hymen aspire. (179 ff.)

But for the sake of good relations with the lieutenant he brushes this aside as unimportant:

Je n'ai pour Aristie aucune répugnance,
Et la Reine à tel point n'asservit pas mon cœur
Qu'il ne fasse encor tout pour le commun bonheur. (206 ff.)

(This is hubris of course, calling for nemesis.) So Perpenna may take Viriate, provided only that she consents:

Dites que vous l'aimez, et je ne l'aime plus [. . .]
Tous mes vœux sont déjà du côté d'Aristie,
Et je l'épouserai, pourvu qu'en même jour
La Reine se résolve à payer votre amour.
Car quoi que vous disiez, je dois craindre sa haine,
Et fuirais à ce prix cette illustre Romaine [Aristie].
(229 ff.)

Aristie appears next, to consult Sertorius on her own problems. Pompée is near the city and is to come under a flag of truce for a conference with his adversary. If this move conceals a wish to take her back, she will forget everything:

Je me dois toute à lui, s'il revient tout à moi. (272)

If not, *la politique* comes first, with a great show of high-minded self-control:

Laissons, Seigneur, laissons pour les petites âmes
Ce commerce rampant de soupirs et de flammes,
Et ne nous unissons que pour mieux soutenir
La liberté que Rome est prête à voir finir.
Unissons ma vengeance à votre politique. [. . .] (285 ff.)

But there is no hurry: better not marry in haste to repent at leisure:

Comme en cet hymen l'amour n'a point de part,
Qu'il n'est qu'un pur effet de noble politique,
Souffrez que je vous die, afin que je m'explique,
Que quand j'aurais pour dot un million de bras,
Je vous donne encor plus en ne l'achevant pas. [. . .]

Ainsi par mon hymen vous avez assurance
Que mille vrais Romains prendront votre défense.
Mais si j'en romps l'accord pour lui rendre mes voeux,
Vous aurez ces Romains et Pompée avec eux . . . (328 ff.)

All the principal threads in the play have now been introduced, though there are more details to be revealed to overload a rather complex situation. D'Aubignac was not wrong – five characters in this kind of play are too many. Besides Pompée, whose perplexities are on the whole the least and who makes only two appearances, Perpenna is given less attention than he needs, and is hard to understand as a result. If a diagram in the manner of Daniel Mornet will help 'new readers', here it is:

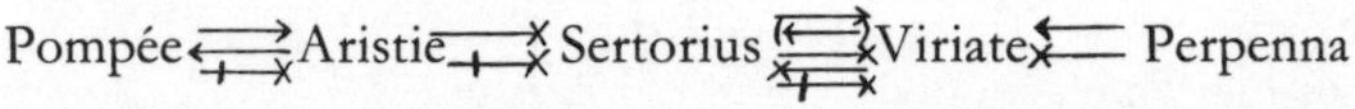

Pompée ⇄ Aristie ⇄ Sertorius ⇄ Viriate ← Perpenna

(where → indicates love, —x a politic plan of marriage, and +—x refusal to marry, at least just yet).

The first lines of the act had voiced the confused sentiments of Perpenna:

D'où me vient ce désordre, Aufide, et que veut dire
Que mon cœur sur mes vœux garde si peu d'empire? (1 ff.)

The last lines are the complaint of Sertorius, revealing a passion that had not appeared before:

Que c'est un sort cruel d'aimer par politique,
Et que ses intérêts sont d'étranges malheurs
S'ils font donner la main quand le cœur est ailleurs!
(370 ff.)

Viriate dominates Act II. We must assume, though we are not told so, that she is young and beautiful, if only because there must be one such part in the cast. But she is a dignified and astute monarch, and she is the only character who does not allow herself to be driven to disclose her private desires. According to her,

Ce ne sont pas les sens que mon amour consulte,
Il hait des passions l'impétueux tumulte,
Et son feu, que j'attache aux soins de ma grandeur,
Dédaigne tout mélange avec leur folle ardeur. (401 ff.)

Stegmann is sure of the contrary, and calls her an 'ardente et pudique amoureuse'.[3] I think all modern readers agree; but Corneille swore she spoke the truth,[4] and d'Aubignac believed her.[5]

When Sertorius comes to speak for Perpenna, she determines to force him then and there to express the sentiments she has already guessed:

S. Si donc je vous offrais pour époux un Romain . . .
V. Pourrais-je refuser un don de votre main?
S. J'ose après cet aveu vous faire offre d'un homme
Digne d'être avoué de l'ancienne Rome [. . .]
Il est couvert de gloire, il est plein de valeur [. . .]
Libéral, intrépide, affable, magnanime,
Enfin, c'est Perpenna sur qui vous emportez . . .
V. J'attendais votre nom après ces qualités [. . .]
Mais certes le détour est un peu surprenant:
Vous donnez une reine à votre lieutenant! (503 ff.)

She goes on to attack him at some length, on every ground of political expediency, like a true Cornelian woman in love; but for the heavier touch, she would remind one of a Marivaux heroine. A lovely scene, not in the least tragic; but perhaps we should ask ourselves why we think it ought to be. At last she calls for Perpenna; and Sertorius in leaving betrays, half willingly, half piteously, his ill-kept secret.

Faites, faites entrer ce héros d'importance,
Que je fasse un essai de mon obéissance,
Et si vous le craignez, craignez autant du moins
Un long et vain regret d'avoir prêté vos soins.
S. Madame, croiriez-vous . . .
V. Ce mot doit vous suffire.
J'entends ce qu'on me dit, et ce qu'on me veut dire.
Allez, faites-lui place, et ne présumez pas . . .
S. Je parle pour un autre, et toutefois, hélas!
Si vous saviez . . .
V. Seigneur, que faut-il que je sache,
Et quel est le secret que ce soupir me cache?
S. Ce soupir redoublé . . .
V. N'achevez point, allez:
Je vous obéirai plus que vous ne voulez. (661 ff.)

Perpenna is then dismissed with the task of proving his submissiveness by ridding Viriate of the threat of Aristie's near presence, who as a Roman and Sertorius' wife (if she took that place) would outrank even the queen, at least in Roman eyes (compare César on this subject, *Pompée* 1069–70).

La politique dominates Act III. The 210 lines of the 'conférence' between the two Roman adversaries Sertorius and Pompée are a justly famous set piece, embodying a profound view of the confusion of moral issues in a civil war. I shall not quote them, for they are strictly a digression; more relevant to the action of the play is the interview of the estranged couple which follows. Aristie, who has found reasons for temporizing over the marriage she had offered Sertorius, is outraged to hear Pompée take the same line with her. He still loves her, but she must wait:

> Ah! ne vous lassez point d'aimer et d'être aimée.
> Peut-être touchons-nous au moment désiré
> Qui saura réunir ce qu'on a séparé.
> Ayez plus de courage et moins d'impatience:
> Souffrez que Sylla meure, ou quitte sa puissance . . .
>
> (1074 ff.)

The public duty which for a hero must outweigh the private claims of love and loyalty is not, now, an action but inaction. Her contempt stings him into threatening to break the truce and fight it out with his rival; they part in bitterness:

> *P.* Eteindre un tel amour!
> *A.* Vous-même l'éteignez.
> . . .
> *P.* Pourrez-vous me haïr?
> *A.* J'en fais tous mes souhaits.
> *P.* Adieu donc pour deux jours.
> *A.* Adieu pour tout jamais.
>
> (1156 ff.)

Nothing comes of all this, but it preludes a third case of unheroic procrastination, this time in Sertorius himself. The theme is one of the ironic or comic substrata of the whole play.

Act IV contains Sertorius' final humiliation, on which Butler bases his whole case; Voltaire had detested the act for the constant intrusion into it of what he calls comedy or irony. Corneille must have spent great pains on its ebb and flow of feeling.

The Roman is first received by Viriate's confidant, who obviously has been briefed to bring him to the point, and does so very deftly. He talks with embarrassment of his reluctant advocacy of Perpenna, in which however, he protests, he had proposed nothing –

capable de me nuire,
Ou qu'un soupir échappé ne dût soudain détruire,
Mais la Reine, sensible à de nouveaux désirs,
Entendait mes raisons, et non pas mes soupirs.
Thamire. Seigneur, quand un Romain, quand un héros soupire,
Nous n'entendons pas bien ce qu'un soupir veut dire [. . .]
S. Ah! pour être Romain, je n'en suis pas moins homme:
J'aime, et peut-être plus qu'on n'a jamais aimé;
Malgré mon âge et moi, mon cœur s'est enflammé.
J'ai cru pouvoir me vaincre, et toute mon adresse
Dans mes plus grands efforts m'a fait voir ma faiblesse.
Ceux [les efforts] de la politique et ceux de l'amitié
M'ont mis en un état à me faire pitié.
Le souvenir m'en tue . . . (1181 ff., 1193 ff.)

So Viriate appears, announcing her complete readiness to marry Perpenna and let Sertorius marry Aristie, the very next day: 'Ce n'est pas obéir qu'obéir lentement . . .' (1228), (in this play, any willingness to act promptly is a bluff). She brushes aside a stammered objection, 'Mes prières pouvaient souffrir quelques refus' (1231), and the wretched man finds no alternative but to speak of dying (1239 ff.). Having now got him where she wants him, she attacks. His reaction to her marriage with Perpenna, she says,

tient moins d'un ami qu'il ne fait d'un rival,
Vous trouvez ma faveur et trop prompte et trop pleine!
L'hymen où je m'apprête est pour vous une gêne!
Vous m'en parlez enfin comme si vous m'aimiez!
S. Souffrez, après ce mot, que je meure à vos pieds.
J'y veux bien immoler tout mon bonheur au vôtre,
Mais je ne vous puis voir entre les bras d'un autre,
Et c'est assez vous dire à quelle extrémité
Me réduit mon amour que j'ai mal écouté. (1252 ff.)

He brings out all his excuses – his age, Aristie, Perpenna, an illusion of *générosité*:

Je m'étais figuré que de tels déplaisirs
Pourraient ne me coûter que deux ou trois soupirs,
Et pour m'en consoler j'envisageais l'estime
Et d'ami généreux et de chef magnanime;
Mais près d'un coup fatal, je sens par mes ennuis
Que je me promettais bien plus que je ne puis . . . (1275 ff.)

Does she love Perpenna? he asks anxiously. She refuses, as always, to admit that she loves at all (the laws of love permit a woman to get away with this untruth where a man cannot).

> Je ne sais que c'est d'aimer ni de haïr,
> Et la part que tantôt vous aviez dans mon âme
> Fut un don de ma gloire, et non pas de ma flamme.
> Je n'en ai point pour lui, je n'en ai point pour vous:
> Je ne veux point d'amant, mais je veux un époux,
> Mais je veux un héros, qui par son hyménée
> Sache élever si haut le trône où je suis née
> Qu'il puisse de l'Espagne être l'heureux soutien,
> Et laisser de vrais rois de mon sang et du sien.
> Je le trouvais en vous, n'eût été la bassesse
> Qui pour ce cher rival contre moi s'intéresse [. . .]
> Je l'oublierai pourtant, et veux vous faire grâce.
> M'aimez-vous? (1284 ff.)

The brilliance of her victory does much, for me, to compensate the ignominy of his defeat. But the victory is not complete. Sertorius is still a *politique*, and cannot accept his happiness at once:

> Ah! Madame, est-il temps que cette grâce éclate?
> *V.* C'est cet éclat, Seigneur, que cherche Viriate.
> *S.* Nous perdons tout, Madame, à le précipiter:
> L'amour de Perpenna le fera révolter.
> Souffrez qu'un peu de temps doucement le ménage,
> Qu'auprès d'un autre objet un autre amour l'engage.
> Des amis d'Aristie assurons le secours
> A force de promettre, en différant toujours . . . (1309 ff.)

Viriate is frank in disavowing any part in these motives – Rome means nothing to her, she wants to detach Sertorius from it. Stegmann sees her carrying here 'l'égoïsme du bonheur à deux jusqu'au blasphème'.[6] All she says is that she wants him for the safety and glory of her kingdom: otherwise, 'Je vais penser à moi, vous penserez à vous' (1395). On that note they part, and it is for the last time.

Sertorius' capitulation was not even as near as we may have thought. He now has to meet Perpenna before he has recovered his composure; they talk for some time, utterly at cross purposes – 'C'est Arnolphe et le notaire', says Butler. At last Perpenna asks about Viriate, and Sertorius tries to tell him that *he* has not changed, but she still will not have him (Perpenna):

Non, je vous l'ai cédée, et vous tiendrai parole.
Je l'aime, et vous la donne encor malgré mon feu,
Mais je crains que ce don n'ait jamais son aveu,
Qu'il n'attire sur nous d'impitoyables haines.
Que vous dirai-je enfin? L'Espagne a d'autres reines . . .

(1478)

Any Corneille character knows how to say yes and mean no. We may think we understand this evasion; though Donneau de Visé in 1663 actually took it for a heroic renunciation.[7] Perpenna shows great emotion, but appears to give way:

Je dois donc me contraindre, et j'y suis résolu.
Oui, sur tous mes désirs je me rends absolu:
J'en veux, à votre exemple, être aujourd'hui le maître,
Et malgré cet amour que j'ai laissé trop croître,
Vous direz à la Reine . . .
S. Eh bien! je lui dirai?
P. Rien, Seigneur, rien encor; demain j'y penserai.

(1515ff.)

However, before the morrow he kills his leader in a banquet, letting him off the hook in the only satisfactory way that was left. His own odious attempt to reap the benefit is quickly put down by the prompt and magnanimous action of Pompée, who restores all that can now be restored; the more easily since his second wife is now dead and Sylla has abdicated.

This last act does something to reinstate the heroic atmosphere. Viriate, Pompée, even Aristie, have had satisfactory and at times impressive parts, facing their private sentimental problems firmly, sometimes with ingenuity and always without dishonour. Sertorius has failed; he has also, at rare moments, been grotesque, at least in modern eyes. 'Souffrez, après ce mot, que je meure à vos pieds' (1256) ought to have been a dramatic climax, and is something else. Corneille is not at ease in such language – not yet: there will be *Suréna*. But here Rotrou could perhaps have done better. Nevertheless, if we are forced to smile must we also despise the hero with feet of clay? What is wrong in tragedy with the hero with feet of clay? May we not, should we not, pity his distress? Have we here a blemish, or an original and daring experiment of the playwright (who promises us 'la nouveauté de quelques caractères' in his *Avis au Lecteur*)? Does the humiliation of Sertorius the personage damn *Sertorius* the play?

True, Corneille never offers another failed hero of this hubristic type again. His next tragedy, *Sophonisbe*, is full of vigorous positive action, to which he calls attention in his foreword. Perhaps he sensed that he had caused disappointment, however little it may have been manifested; that the most faithful of his partisans still saw him as the Corneille of 1640, and were still looking, like Butler, for a lot more Horaces.

But is this perhaps an instance of his love of paradox, of surprise, of the aesthetic of *éblouissement* in which P. France sees the secret of his art?[8]

In *Sertorius*, there is not only the sad shock of the hero who imposes a test on himself and fails: there are not one, but three supposedly heroic characters who upset the man or woman who agrees to marry them by pleading for time – and, to delay, Sertorius proposes to add deliberate deception; and there is the 'vieillard amoureux' who, as Créuse had told us long before (*Medée* 538) 'mérite qu'on en rie'.

Not all Corneille's bold strokes came off; we shall come across this tendency of his again. For all his professed desire to please, he was sublimely indifferent to public taste if it failed to meet his own. Perhaps with *Sertorius* he was anxious to see how his public would react to such a change of moral atmosphere, when he gave them a deficiency of heroism, instead of the excess they expected. If so, he was disappointed. No one seems to have noticed.

Othon: the unheroic hero

In *Othon*, rather similarly, there is a gap where one expected to find the hero. The tragedy lacks any commanding figure (A. Adam), any hero or action that can be called tragic (A. Stegmann), all moral fibre and authenticity of character (S. Doubrovsky). It cannot quite be called *le degré zéro du tragique*, if Stegmann and Doubrovsky are right to see glimmers of true tragedy in the most pitiful moments of failure it displays.[9]

I should be content to call it the zero of Cornelian heroism – meaning that self-confident courage based on self-mastery, the 'joyeux élan et l'éclat lumineux vers lequel courait le héros',[10] which many critics see as the poet's characteristic note, and remembering that in 1644 he had been happy to equate the two words *héroïque* and *tragique*.[11] For this Othon inspires in us, certainly not admiration, but something so much nearer to contempt that it is hard to feel pity or fear on his behalf – harder even than it was with Sertorius. The most one can plead for him – and I shall make the plea – is that his irresolution, his helplessness, his reluctant and unsuccessful deceitfulness, are forced on him by the cage of circumstance in which his creator has imprisoned him, for dramatic purposes which one must try to deduce.

Othon is another Roman play, and more Roman than *Sertorius* and *Sophonisbe* which preceded it, in that it is set in Rome itself. This is a Rome new in Corneille's drama – the festering Rome of corruption, instability and violence left by Nero at his death; the year AD 69 was one of the most agitated in its century. And Corneille had taken up – surprisingly late, since all political thinkers had been using it for years – a historical source new to him. Tacitus recounts the same events at the beginning of his *Histories*, and in even darker colours, charged with all the indignation of a moralist and a Roman patriot.

The picture of Nero's successor, the aged Galba, and his unscrupulous ministers, comes straight out of Tacitus (I.6–7):

> . . . Je fus le premier qu'on vit au nouveau Prince
> Donner toute une armée et toute une province:
> Ainsi je me comptais de ses premiers suivants.
> Mais déjà Vinius avait pris les devants.
> Martian l'affranchi, dont tu vois les pillages,
> Avait avec Lacus fermé tous les passages:
> On n'approchait de lui que sous leur bon plaisir.
> J'eus donc pour m'y produire un des trois à choisir.
> Je les voyais tous trois se hâter sous un maître
> Qui, chargé d'un long âge, a peu de temps à l'être,
> Et tous trois à l'envi s'empresser ardemment
> A qui dévorerait ce règne d'un moment.
> J'eus horreur des appuis qui restaient seuls à prendre,
> J'espérai quelque temps de m'en pouvoir défendre,
> Mais quand Nymphidius, dans Rome assassiné,
> Fit place au favori qui l'avait condamné . . .
>
> . . . .
>
> Je vis qu'il était temps de prendre mes mesures,
> Qu'on perdait de Néron toutes les créatures . . .
>
> . . . .
>
> Je choisis Vinius dans cette défiance,
> Pour plus de sûreté j'en cherchai l'alliance . . .
>
> (33 ff., 53 ff., 57 ff.)

Othon, who speaks these lines, appears in a fairly favourable light; Corneille admits (*Au Lecteur*) that he has cleaned up the portrait he found in the histories. He is high-born, a Senator and ambitious – or he was ambitious until he fell in love – and is now too prominent for it to be safe for him to retire into obscurity. His betrothal was originally an act of calculation.

Ceux qu'on voit s'étonner de ce nouvel amour
N'ont jamais bien conçu ce que c'est que la cour.
Un homme tel que moi jamais ne s'en détache,
Il n'est point de retraite ou d'ombre qui le cache,
Et si du souverain la faveur n'est pour lui
Il faut, ou qu'il périsse, ou qu'il prenne un appui.

(15 ff.)

But Othon is rehabilitated by Corneille only just enough to make him a little more desirable than his rival Pison, whom we never see, and of whom we are told almost nothing, except that as Emperor he will be easy to lead by the nose (645 f.: a detail not borne out by Tacitus or any other historian, all of whom think him the better candidate). Othon's record as governor of Lusitania (to which he had been relegated) is his one good point, his life as boon-companion of Néron and husband of Poppée is excused but by no means forgotten. However he is unassuming, he strikes no attitudes, he suffers when he is forced into insincerity. He has lost his ambition:

Vous voulez que je règne, et je ne sais qu'aimer.
Je pourrais savoir plus, si l'astre qui domine
Me voulait faire un jour régner avec Plautine . . .

(244 ff.)

– and Corneille varies his stage-lighting from play to play so often that I find it impossible to judge whether this counts as a black mark or a saving grace.

For this is where the other factor comes in – the love interest. It will constitute the cage into which the hapless Othon steps as early as Act I, Scene 4. As in so many Cornelian plays, this interest is hung on a historical peg that only a keen eye could have discerned. Vinius, according to Tacitus and other writers, had a daughter whom he wished to marry to Othon in order to bind the young senator to him. Corneille notes (*Au Lecteur*) that in history the marriage never took place. We learn later in the *Histories* (I. 47) that her name was Crispina; but, as nobody notices her name there, Corneille seems to feel free to call her what he likes. Plautine has a rival; for Galba, who cannot live much longer and is childless, is expected to leave the throne to the man who marries his niece Camille; and Camille, as we learn and Vinius knows, is partial to Othon. She would provide an easier and surer route than Plautine could, for Othon to reach the rank he covets, or once coveted.

The crisis which forms the *nœud* of the play is precisely this: that the two other ministers are blocking the Othon–Plautine match, which would make Vinius too powerful, and are, Vinius says, threatening his life and those of his daughter and Othon. Othon must save them and himself at once, in the only way possible: 'gagner Camille' (169). He would rather die; but Plautine joins her father:

> Il faut vivre, et l'amour nous y doit obliger,
> Pour me sauver un père, et pour me protéger.
> Quand vous voyez ma vie à la vôtre attachée
> Faut-il que malgré moi votre âme effarouchée
> Pour m'ouvrir le tombeau hâte votre trépas
> Et m'avance un destin où je ne consens pas?
>
> (299 ff.)

Though Voltaire in his commentary pooh-poohs this motive, finding the danger much exaggerated,[12] it is the mainspring of the dramatic action, and it seems we are meant to take it in deadly earnest.

Camille, and the whole complication built up on her existence, are downright inventions of Corneille. He gives himself complete freedom, from this point to the violent denouement (and that, as we shall see, is pretty free also) to spin out of his own imagination a web of matrimonial intrigue to serve as the accompaniment, or the translation into stage terms, of a complicated power-struggle.

It is the price of this pattern-weaving that AD 69, the Year of the Three Emperors (Galba, Otho, Vitellius), the crisis of the Roman Principate, is shown to us here rather as the ballet of the eight or nine marriages, all invented and none realized, fruits of the 'intrigues de cabinet qui se détruisent les unes les autres', of which the poet seems actually to boast in his foreword. For Othon's switch to Camille is only the beginning of the ballet, other matches will be talked of: Camille is to marry Pison, the other candidate for the throne; Pison is to marry Plautine; Plautine is to be given to Martian the freedman, all in view of somebody's political advantage, by calculations that the reader has not always time to grasp, and which there is no possibility of enumerating and explaining here. Galba reels off the whole list, to convince his niece of what he takes to be the inexhaustible compliance of Vinius, Plautine's father:

Vinius par son zèle est trop justifié:
Voyez ce qu'en un jour il m'a sacrifié.
Il m'offre Othon pour vous, qu'il souhaitait pour gendre,
Je le rends à sa fille, il aime à le reprendre,
Je la veux pour Pison, mon vouloir est suivi,
Je vous mets en sa place, et l'en trouve ravi,
Son ami se révolte, il presse ma colère,
Il donne à Martian Plautine à ma prière:
Et je soupçonnerais un crime dans les vœux
D'un homme qui s'attache à tout ce que je veux?

(1507 ff.)

To return to the first Act. Othon, protesting vainly, is shut into his cage, less by Vinius than by Plautine herself, who demands a renunciation to match her own:

Tout ce que vous sentez, je le sens dans mon âme,
J'ai mêmes déplaisirs, comme j'ai même flamme,
J'ai mêmes désespoirs, mais je sais les cacher
Et paraître insensible afin de moins toucher.
Faites à vos désirs pareille violence . . .

. . . .

Suivez, passez l'example, et portez à Camille
Un visage content, un visage tranquille,
Qui lui laisse accepter ce que vous offrirez,
Et ne démente rien de ce que vous direz.

Othon Hélas, Madame, hélas! que pourrai-je lui dire?

Plautine Il y va de ma vie, il y va de l'Empire.

(345 ff., 357 ff.)

There is no 'heroic' way out of this, certainly no question of dying sword in hand in her defence. 'L'unique sacrifice généreux' in the matrimonial plays, as Stegmann has said, is 'donner la main sans le cœur'.[13] Sertorius had tried to do the same thing, though he had not had to parade a love he did not feel. A later hero to experience Othon's predicament will be Racine's Bajazet, forced by Atalide to appease and reassure the Sultana who holds both their lives in her hand (and certain details suggest Racine had *Othon* in the back of his mind); and

Bajazet, like Othon, has been judged spineless for not taking action he could not take. Later in the play, Bajazet does act differently, and regains thereby much of our respect.

Othon is allowed only two actions. The first is to offer his hand to Camille: the second is to back out as quickly and gracefully as he can – quickly rather than gracefully – when, almost immediately, the aged Galba, who is just a little less feeble-minded than they think him, amuses himself and punishes his niece for trying to reject Pison, by giving Camille to Othon but the throne to Pison. Each action of Othon is the subject of a striking scene. The first (II. 1) is, like the comparable scene in Bajazet (III. 1–2), simply a *récit*, which in fact, in the mouth of Plautine's Flavie – a confidant as observant and witty as Viriate's Thamire – tells us more than the painful spectacle of Othon's lying would have done. She does not dwell on his hypocrisy (she is reporting to Plautine, who had forced him into it) but on his clumsiness, his lack of the ease and air of spontaneity which are expected of any lover and any *honnête homme*:

> Son éloquence accorte, enchaînant avec grâce
> L'excuse du silence à celle de l'audace,
> En termes trop choisis accusait le respect
> D'avoir tant retardé cet hommage suspect.
> Ses gestes concertés, ses regards de mesure
> N'y laissaient aucun mot aller à l'aventure . . .
> Jusque dans ses soupirs la justesse régnait . . .
>
> (401 ff.)

Camille is taken in for the moment, but only because she wants to be.

> Elle aurait mieux goûté des discours moins suivis,
> Je l'ai vu dans ses yeux, mais cette défiance
> Avait avec son cœur trop peu d'intelligence . . .
> Elle a voulu tout croire . . .
> . . . elle prenait plaisir à se laisser tromper.
>
> (412 ff.)

The second scene (III. 5) is played out in front of us. This time Camille's eyes are wide open; but she fights on, refuting his excuses, trying to prove that the Empire will still eventually be his (since she thinks he attaches a value to it that she does not). She wants this inadequate hero, and has made great (if unforeseen) sacrifices to get him. It does not occur to Othon to make a clean breast and throw himself on her mercy; no doubt he fears for Plautine, and also for himself.

Quoi donc, Madame, Othon vous coûterait
 l'Empire?
Il sait mieux ce qu'il vaut, et n'est pas d'un tel prix
Qu'il le faille acheter par ce noble mépris . . .
. . . .
Ah! Madame, quittez cette vaine espérance
De nous voir quelque jour remettre en la balance.
S'il faut que de Pison on accepte la loi
Rome, tant qu'il vivra, n'aura plus d'yeux pour
 moi . . .
Il n'est point ni d'exil, ni de Lusitanie
Qui dérobe à Pison le reste de ma vie . . .

Camille Et c'est là ce grand coeur qu'on croyait intrépide!
Le péril, comme un autre, à mes yeux l'intimide! . . .
Il redoute Pison! Dites-moi donc, de grâce . . .
Etes-vous moins rivaux pour ne m'épouser pas? . . .
[Il] peut tout contre vous, à moins que contre lui
Mon hymen chez Galba vous assure un appui.

Othon Eh bien! il me perdra pour vous avoir aimée,
Sa haine sera douce à mon âme enflammée,
Et tout mon sang n'a rien que je veuille épargner
Si ce n'est que par là que vous pouvez régner.
(1030 ff., 1057 ff., 1089 ff., 1103 ff.)

'Le tragique propre d'*Othon* vient de ce que tous les personnages parlent le language cornélien de la générosité . . . et mentent', comments Stegmann.[14] (Not all, perhaps; Camille comes out well from the contrast.) Corneille has for once refused to lend one of his characters his gift of plausible advocacy; but what makes Othon's resistance so paltry and unconvincing is precisely his sense of his false position – what remains to him of integrity and loyalty.

He has only one other considerable scene (IV. 1). He runs straight from Camille to Plautine (though his confidant tries to keep him away, 1150) to make an abject exhibition of his helplessness; asking her advice (and when did a Cornelian hero do this until now?), having no idea of his next move, talking repeatedly about death (but doing nothing about that), and inviting her to die with him, refusing to make any attempt to appease Camille. Eventually Plautine promises (or threatens) to accept the marriage offered by Martian, the most repulsive of Galba's ministers (a freedman, so presumably a barbarian), in order to obtain his support for Othon: even this only provokes more talk of suicide –

> *Othon* En concevez-vous bien toute l'ignominie?
> *Plautine* Je n'en puis voir, Seigneur, à vous sauver la vie.
> *Othon* L'épouser à ma vue! et pour comble d'ennui . . .
> *Plautine* Donnez-vous à Camille, ou je me donne à lui.
> *Othon* Périssons, périssons, Madame, l'un pour l'autre,
> Avec toute ma gloire, avec toute la vôtre . . .
>
> (1233 ff.)

Or at least, he adds, let her find someone decent to sacrifice herself to:

> . . . ne me préférez qu'un illustre rival.
> J'en mourrai de douleur, mais je mourrais de rage
> Si vous me préfériez un reste d'esclavage.
>
> (1244 ff.)

It is a beautiful dramatic irony that at this very moment Vinius comes in (IV. 2) to tell him that the throne is his for the taking, if only he will be quick: there has been an opportune mutiny. But Othon is not even capable of being quick, and is pushed unceremoniously out in a 'fuite en avant', to become 'Empereur malgré lui'.[15]

> Seigneur,
> Vous empêcherez tout, si vous avez du cœur.
> Malgré de nos destins la rigueur importune,
> Le ciel met en vos mains toute notre fortune . . .
> Courez donc à la place, où vous les trouverez [the mutineers],
> Suivez-les dans leur camp, et vous en assurez,
> Un temps bien pris peut tout.
> *Othon* Si cet astre contraire
> Qui m'a .
> *Vinius* Sans discourir faites ce qu'il faut faire:
> Un moment de séjour peut tout déconcerter,
> Et le moindre soupçon vous va faire arrêter.
> *Othon* Avant que de partir souffrez que je proteste . . .
> *Vinius* Partez, en Empereur vous nous direz le reste.
>
> (1247 ff., 1275 ff.)

This is the last we see of him till the last scene of the tragedy. The fifth act is exciting with its suspense and its reversals (we are told Corneille rewrote it three times);[16] though it makes a surprising and inappropriate ending for a play of inadequacy and failure.[17] Othon is in the thick of the action . . . doing nothing. On the stage talk goes on about the marriages; in the intervals news arrives from outside – that Othon is proclaimed emperor by a few troops, 'carried' to the guards' camp, finally murdered by order of Martian. But this is a lie, to throw his opponents off their guard. Pison, Martian, Vinius, Galba, Lacus, die off-stage in turn, by various hands, but not his.[18] Here Corneille commits the most serious of his violations of history; for Tacitus and the other historians leave no doubt that this was a treacherous coup engineered by Otho himself against the man he had helped to put on the throne, and that he himself ordered the killing of Piso (*Histories* I. 44). Corneille keeps his hero's hands clean at the cost of showing him no less inert in a revolution than in a boudoir. He returns when all his enemies have been eliminated, to say only that he regards himself as responsible for Plautine's father's death and will continue to do nothing, will not even appear before the Senate, unless Plautine approves, and that he means to be kind to Camille.

We can only wonder what these two had seen in him; either of them is worth two of him. They are a finely contrasted pair, each endowed with some of the heroic virtues.

Camille has something of the old Cornelian self-assertion against all the odds. She puts the all-powerful ministers, her father's rivals, in their place with an assurance that conceals its lack of foundation:

> Faut-il vous dire encor que j'ai des yeux ouverts?
> Je vois jusqu'en vos cœurs, et m'obstine à me taire,
> Mais je pourrais enfin dévoiler le mystère.
> *Martian* Si l'Empereur nous croit . . .
> *Camille* Sans doute il vous croira,
> Sans doute je prendrai l'époux qu'il m'offrira:
> Soit qu'il plaise à mes yeux, soit qu'il me choque en l'âme,
> Il sera votre maître, et je serai sa femme.
> Le temps me donnera sur lui quelque pouvoir,
> Et vous pourrez alors vous en apercevoir.
> Voilà les quatre mots que j'avais à vous dire.
> Pensez-y.

(740 ff.)

More dutiful than her namesake in *Horace*, she is nearly as obstinate with her uncle, but with grace and wit. She will let herself be sacrificed in the last resort, but not if she can help it.

> Ce n'est pas qu'après tout je pense à résister:
> J'aime à vous obéir, Seigneur, sans contester.
> Pour prix d'un sacrifice où mon cœur se dispose,
> Permettez qu'un époux me doive quelque chose.
> Dans cette servitude où se plaît mon désir,
> C'est quelque liberté qu'un ou deux à choisir.
> Votre Pison peut-être aura de quoi me plaire,
> Quand il ne sera plus un mari nécessaire . . . (927 ff.)

Unlike so many of her Cornelian sisters – most unlike Domitie in a later play, but like Othon – she cares nothing if she has to lose the Empire for her love. Like all Corneille's women she is cruelly spiteful to her rival, and the scene of their confrontation (IV. 4) is the bitterest such scene he wrote. The revenge she plots with Martian (IV. 5) is appalling – Othon is to be assassinated, but only after he has seen his Plautine united to the freedman; however, we learn, in almost her last scene (IV. 6), that this was a subterfuge, the only way she can see of saving Othon, who will be able to escape (1470). Plautine is not mentioned: her punishment presumably is not revoked.

Stegmann, who is charmed by Camille,[19] surprises me by overlooking Plautine, whose virtues are boundless loyalty and self-sacrifice. Where Camille gives up *gloire* for love, Plautine asks only the *gloire* of making Othon Emperor (325 ff.). She immolates herself twice: once by sending Othon to Camille, and once in her offer to marry Martian – Martian whom she loathes and despises (see her earlier rejection of him, II.2), not mainly because he is grasping and unprincipled (like her father! but children do not take after their parents in Corneille) but because he had been 'l'esclave Icélus', 'Qu'il a changé de nom sans changer de visage' (493). (Her violent social prejudice offends us, as it offended Voltaire:[20] but it is simply the converse of the *préjugé nobiliaire* we have learnt to excuse.)

These two female roles are far less inert than Othon's, and nearly as long: Othon is present in ten scenes, Plautine in thirteen, Camille in twelve; each speaks between 250 and 300 lines. Was not one of them more worthy than he is of the title role, like Sophonisbe or Pulchérie? But, apart from the fact that they have no political designs for themselves, they have one insuperable disqualification – one at least that is never overridden in any tragedy to my knowledge: they have no historical background. (This is one of the dramatic rules that I think I may claim to have discovered: that no character's name may appear on the title-page of a tragedy unless his or her papers are in order.) Moreover, though literature and especially fiction were much less male-chauvinist than real-life society in the seventeenth century, Corneille's choice of matrimonial plots seems to invite us to look for docility, 'la gloire d'obéir', in the *filles à marier*, and initiative in the battling males.

Sophonisbe: patriotism and jealousy

The strikingly different play *Sophonisbe* which divides (chronologically) these two cases of moral feebleness has necessarily been omitted until now. Sophonisba, is, of course, the African queen much favoured by Renaissance playwrights for having found the time, in the space of twenty-four hours, to be the wife of two different men and to take poison as well. She was the subject of the first French new-style tragedy. Corneille seems to have chosen the subject (in 1663) less for the advantage of having Mairet's work (of 1634) as a model, than to take the opposite course as often as possible. He explains in his Foreword what may have been a new doctrine, but one quite in conformity with practice in regard to imitation of contemporaries. He has, he says, avoided borrowing any details from Mairet's characters or plot, though he uses their common source. Mairet's heroine had been a tragic personage, blackened only slightly by infidelity to her aged husband, Syphax, to whom she had been linked by a forced marriage. Her dangerous and devouring patriotism for Carthage hardly shows up, though the Romans know it and fear it. Corneille gives us, instead of her, a heroine, if she is one, rather in the style of Medée, Cléopâtre or Arsinoé; sacrificing herself and everyone around her – so she says – to the respectable motive of patriotism. She is a virago who upstages the warrior Massinisse almost as completely as she dominates her husband Syphax. 'Je lui prête un peu d'amour', says Corneille in his *Au Lecteur* – indeed after refusing Massinisse anything but the bare ceremony of marriage on the grounds of her urgent danger of becoming a captive, she bids him farewell with a coy avowal which would not have disgraced any heroine of the '*tragédie galante*':

> Adieu. Ce qui m'échappe en faveur de vos feux
> Est moins que je ne sens, et plus que je ne veux.
>
> (1507 f.)

'. . . mais elle règne sur lui [cet amour] et ne daigne l'écouter qu'autant qu'il peut servir à ces passions dominantes qui règnent sur elle, et à qui elle sacrifie toutes les tendresses de son cœur.' And so indeed it seems at first blush and to the outside world. Her acts, and her words almost, are without sentiment. She is without pity for the husband she has pushed into defeat and who, far from dying on the field as Mairet and his predecessors had thought it proper to make him, survives in chains to be repudiated by her (1049–52), and in revenge to alert the Roman victors to his wife's doings (1213 ff.). There will be more to say about her motives in seducing Massinisse to marry her. She rejects the gift of poison, after Massinisse has failed to obtain her release (as related in the sources), with defiant contempt:

> Reportez, Mézétulle, à votre illustre Roi
> Un secours dont lui-même a plus besoin que moi:
> Il ne manquera pas d'en faire un digne usage,
> Dès qu'il aura des yeux à voir son esclavage.
> Si tous les rois d'Afrique en sont toujours pourvus
> Pour dérober leur gloire aux malheurs imprévus,
> Comme eux et comme lui j'en dois être munie,
> Et quand il me plaira de sortir de la vie,
> De montrer qu'une femme a plus de cœur que lui,
> On ne me verra point emprunter rien d'autrui.
>
> (1605 ff.)

The excuse offered for this almost unvarying insensibility is always a passionate loyalty she feels for Carthage. In fact, as once she confesses to her confidant, her recapture of Massinisse, her most significant exploit and, as she thinks, the miscalculation most likely to have caused her downfall, was explained by love – or rather by that jealousy Corneille seems to have considered as inseparable from love. He often shows us a woman in love (or having had a suitor) utterly refusing to consent to let him know happiness, if separated from her, with any alternative partner, unless of her own choosing, to demonstrate her power over a lover even when she cannot keep him. This may be done as a sign of overpowering affection, as when Eurydice withholds consent from the marriage that would save the life of Suréna. Sophonisbe had made her husband offer his sister to Massinisse (who rejected the offer):

> *Herminie* Ce fut, s'il m'en souvient, votre prière expresse
> Qui lui fit par Syphax offrir cette princesse,

Et je ne puis trouver matière à vos douleurs
Dans la perte d'un cœur que vous donniez ailleurs.

Sophonisbe Je le donnais, ce cœur où ma rivale aspire:
Ce don, s'il l'eût souffert, eût marqué monempire,
Eût montré qu'un amant si maltraité par moi
Prenait encor plaisir à recevoir ma loi.
Après m'avoir perdue, il aurait fait connaître
Qu'il voulait m'être encor tout ce qu'il pouvait m'être,
Se rattacher à moi par les liens du sang,
Et tenir de ma main la splendeur de son rang.
Mais s'il épouse Eryxe, il montre un coeur rebelle
Qui me néglige autant qu'il veut brûler pour elle,
Qui brise tous mes fers, et brave hautement
L'éclat de sa disgrâce et de mon changement.

Herminie Certes, si je l'osais je nommerais caprice
Ce trouble ingénieux à vous faire un supplice,
Et l'obstination des soucis superflus
Dont vous gêne ce cœur quand vous n'en voulez plus.

Sophonisbe Ah! que de notre orgueil tu sais mal la faiblesse,
Quand tu veux que son choix n'ait rien qui m'intéresse!. . .
Des cœurs que la vertu renonce à posséder,
La conquête toujours semble douce à garder:
Sa rigueur [celle de la vertu] n'a jamais le dehors si sévère,
Que leur perte au-dedans ne lui devienne amère;
Et de quelque façon qu'elle nous fasse agir,
Un esclave échappé nous fait toujours rougir.

(103 ff.)

This speech occurs in the second scene of the play, so Corneille has given fair warning of his heroine's propensities. When she snatched her old lover from under the very nose of his more recently betrothed Eryxe, it was a wild, spontaneous reaction – of spite not of love.

Herminie Mais vous lui témoigniez pareille impatience,
Et vos feux rallumés montraient de leur côté
Pour ce nouvel hymen égale avidite.
Sophonisbe Ce n'etait point l'amour qui la rendait égale.
[égale à l'"avidité' de Massinisse]
C'était la folle ardeur de braver ma rivale.

(1541 ff.)

This then, as H.T. Barnwell[21] has rightly shown, is the cause of her failure, the flaw in her plans; her sudden action had alerted the Romans, who just might have let her alone without it. She herself blames on this all the failure of her hopes. What seems to prove that Corneille designed this act as the mainspring of his catastrophe is the fact that he invented, *de toutes pièces*, the figure of the rival Eryxe, whose name he seems to have taken inappositely from that of a Sicilian mountain, as that of her kingdom, Hiarbée, comes from the name of the suitor of Dido in Virgil. Massinisse had gained her love and her support at a time when the forces of Syphax had left him helpless, but without being permitted to marry her until he was again King in fact.

So our heroine might have perhaps survived, but her efforts, her heroic parade of defiance go for nothing. Her only reward is the tribute of a Roman, 'Une telle fierté devait naître romaine' (1812) and Love appears once more as a counterbalancing force to politics, but Corneille has 'changed the signs' – it is love in an evil, malignant aspect, a deliberately introduced variant in the Cornelian scheme.

VI

Corneille After Corneille

Agésilas: musical chairs

This seems the right point to choose for the beginning of Corneille's decline – unless we see it, as perhaps we should, as being less a failure of imagination or craft, than a refusal to provide (not a failure to realize) what his public looked for. It is not only that he never again (after *Attila*) will score a full success; but that, as if symbolically, this is the date at which he meets the young upstart Racine on his path. Hostility seems to have been mutual: Corneille had never much minded or resented the rivalry of his brother or Quinault, though he may have objected on grounds of taste to these *doucereux* and *enjoués*. In Racine he seems to have been prescient enough to see a real challenge.

The year of *Othon* – 1664 – was also the year of *La Thébaïde*. *Agésilas* followed *Alexandre* in 1666, and must have suffered somewhat from the clash, for though *La Thebaïde* had been negligible as competition, *Alexandre* was just what the century liked and expected – a thoroughly well composed and well written play (though devoid of tragic substance), probably better than anything Thomas Corneille or Quinault could produce. Hostility between the two great poets was marked by the time of *Britannicus* – Racine accused Corneille of ill will in his Preface, and attacked him for the *invraisemblances* in his characterization. The quarrel over the two *Bérénices* the year after was a pitched battle, which will have to be examined.

What is not clear is why Corneille gives up at this point ending his plays (whether 'tragédies' or 'comédies héroïques') with a death – returning to the practice only with his last play, *Suréna*. He had done it before in *Cinna* of course, *Nicomède* and *Pertharite*, but danger and the threat of death had been in the air: in *Agésilas* the sense of danger is far less. In the plays that follow now, a political marriage is awaited on which depends the stability of the state, the king (or emperor, or empress regnant) is involved. He (or she) makes the right decision, which is against his own desires; the situation is saved, the denouement is not a death, but a marriage or even a cascade of marriages, as in a comedy. This recurs again in each play (except that in *Attila* there is no decision but the Hun dies by 'natural causes'), up to *Pulchérie*.

It may be that Corneille is aware of giving a milder atmosphere to the plays he is now writing; or he may wish to confer a tragic status on the renunciation of love.

He continues his tacking course, looking for contrasts. *Agésilas* is a *pièce rose*[1] (relatively) beside the sombre *Othon* which it succeeds. *Tite et Bérénice* matches *Agésilas*, but the two are separated, in the triptych pattern we have noted already, by the violently different *Attila*, a work I would gladly pass over if I dared, for I do not understand how it came to be.

Corneille makes great play in the *Au Lecteur* of *Agésilas* with the originality of his form: the poet Horace had praised innovation in Roman playwrights, he says, and 'chacun peut hasarder à ses périls'. *Agésilas* is a *tragédie enjouée*;[2] it would surely have been offered, not as a tragedy but as a *comédie héroïque*, if Corneille had remembered in time that he had invented the term; for it is not true enough to history (the women characters and love interests are all invented), and the hero's 'peril' is not acute. It owes its surprisingly new spirit, at least in part, to a change in metre (this must be the innovation he alludes to) – occasional octosyllables interrupt the steady 6 + 6 of the now familiar rhetoric of Corneille's alexandrine; the rhyme-schemes are varied; the verse is lighter, closer to the movements of the human mind, and only less witty than La Fontaine's freer *vers libre* with its wider gamut of metres. It is equally suited to the defiant flippancy of Aglatide, a high-spirited girl masking the disappointment she is too proud to confess:

> Je sais comme il faut vivre, et m'en trouve fort bien.
> La joie est bonne à mille choses,
> Mais le chagrin n'est bon à rien.
> Ne perds-je pas assez, sans doubler l'infortune,
> Et perdre encor le bien d'avoir l'esprit égal?
> Perte sur perte est importune,
> Et je m'aime un peu trop pour me traiter si mal.
> Soupirer quand le sort nous rend une injustice,
> C'est lui prêter une aide à nous faire un supplice.
> Pour moi, qui ne lui puis souffrir tant de pouvoir,
> Le bien que je me veux met sa haine à pis faire. (839–49)

> Mais je sais ne vouloir que ce qui m'est possible,
> Quand je ne puis ce que je veux. (1555 ff.)

– and to the sometimes ironic, pondered utterances (so unlike Auguste or Pompée) of a statesman king in difficulties with a factious underling:

> A te dire le vrai, l'affaire m'embarrasse:
> J'ai peine à démêler ce qu'il faut que je fasse,
> Tant la confusion de mes raisonnements
> Etonne mes ressentiments.
> Lysander m'a servi: j'aurais une âme ingrate
> Si je méconnaissais ce que je tiens de lui.
> Il a servi l'Etat, et si son crime éclate,
> Il y trouvera de l'appui.
> Je sens que ma reconnaissance
> Ne cherche qu'un moyen de le mettre à couvert,
> Mais enfin il y va de toute ma puissance:
> Si je ne le perds, il me perd.
> Ce que veut l'intérêt, la prudence ne l'ose,
> Tu peux juger par là du désordre où je suis.
>
> (1120–33)

Though ingenious and moving, the play wears a certain air of unreality, due to the interweaving of a serious study of a political problem firmly based on Plutarch, with a romantic story (fictitious, needless to say) of three mismatched pairs of lovers struggling to straighten out their situation.

There is covert struggle between Agésilas, one of the kings of Sparta (the other king has been edited out by Corneille) and the great Spartan admiral Lysander, to whom he owes his throne (by a shady transaction into which Corneille does not enter) and who subsequently tries to usurp all the real power. He is systematically thwarted by the king's action against his subordinates. All this faithfully follows Plutarch, up to the ending (exclusively) in a triumphant reconciliation after a magnanimous refusal to use incriminating evidence (imitated from Pompée in *Sertorius*) which is pure invention: Corneille was not afraid of changing *les effets* as freely as *les acheminements* of his plot when he chose, as witness *Nicomède* (see p. 56). The theme of the over-powerful vassal has been carried to the extreme point where the vassal becomes a real enemy, ready with a plotted *coup d'Etat*; this plot, which looks like a piece of dramatic machinery, is completely authenticated by Plutarch.

Ephesus is the meeting-place chosen for all these characters; it was the Spartan base for the intermittent hostilities against Persia. But we hear nothing of any hostilities, and the moves in the matrimonial tangle take up far more time than matters of state. The malcontent Lysander has betrothed his two daughters to two refugees from that land of tyranny, the East dominated by Persia – a Persian noble Spitridate, and an Asiatic monarch Cotys of Paphlagonia (the names are taken from Plutarch, but from different contexts). But the couples have now met, and discovered that neither is suited. Spitridate loves not Aglatide but her elder sister Elpinice, betrothed to Cotys. A simple exchange would be no help, for Cotys will hear of no one but the Persian Mandane, the sister of Spitridate. Aglatide, who makes a mystery of her real inclinations (which are for Agésilas, who once trifled with her affections, or ambitions), refuses to release a king for any exchange less valuable, and Elpinice abets her. Whereupon Agésilas vetoes the two matches, which would make Lysander too powerful. But then, Cotys has a bargaining counter that should move him: these matrimonial calculations have always attracted Corneille. We remember the 'huit ou neuf mariages proposés pour n'en conclure aucun' in *Othon* (see p. 85). The king has shown strong interest in the Persian's sister Mandane, who is her brother's ward, being an orphan or else too cut-off from any family back at home, and she is, he says,

> trop bien née
> Pour dédire un devoir qui la met sous ma loi. (376)

Offered to Agésilas, she may induce him to relent. She expresses no objection to this utterly cynical intention, perhaps realizing that she cannot go back to Persia, and has little hope in this atmosphere of male political manœuvres; though she is remarkably good at pointing out to the king the dangers he would run in flouting Spartan law by marrying a foreigner (a dress rehearsal, this, for *Tite et Bérénice*). Indeed in a last tense interview (V. 4) she brings up all these considerations and finally makes no secret of her willingness to give her hand but not her heart (1905). This is a piece of frankness I believe to be absolutely without any parallel in Corneille until we find it again in Eurydice (*Suréna*). In drama as in real life, the old tradition had assumed for the sake of convenience that any daughter knew her duty too well to have any inclinations to overcome. To reveal them was immodest in the girl, tactless in the man.

Such a spirited challenge by Mandane fills the king with admiration but leaves him painfully irresolute. His choice of wife, and his way of dealing with Lysander (of whose treason he now has evidence) are both in doubt.

Je n'en suis pas encor d'accord avec moi-même.
J'aime, mais après tout je hais autant que j'aime.
Et ces deux passions qui règnent tour à tour
Ont au fond de mon cœur si peu d'intelligence
Qu'à peine immole-t-il la vengeance à l'amour,
Qu'il voudrait immoler l'amour à la vengeance.

(1937 ff.)

Yet it is evident that he must reach his decision at this moment, though Corneille allows us neither to see him making up his mind, nor to know the result till it becomes apparent, nor even to be sure of his motive. The king clears up the political situation with great firmness and celerity. The solution is a reconciliation, the price he pays is the renunciation of both vengeance and love. He sees Lysander, who has come to express thanks for the permission for Spitridate to marry Elpinice, and confirms that Cotys may have Mandane, though at the price of the king's own sacrifice. Then, without warning, he confronts the admiral in private with the proof of his plotting; promises secrecy and hands over the evidence unexamined, proposing peace:

Dites-moi seulement avec même franchise,
Vous dois-je encor bien plus que vous ne me devez?

(2032 ff.)

(His motive was no doubt to ensure peace for the kingdom; but also marriage with Lysander's daughter would be the only way to fill up the gap in the sentimental musical chairs.) His last words wind up the political issue on a suitably grave note.

Jugez-en comme il faut en juger,
Et surtout commencez d'apprendre
Que les rois sont jaloux du souverain pouvoir,
Qu'ils aiment qu'on leur doive, et ne peuvent devoir,
Que rien à leurs sujets n'acquiert l'indépendance,
Qu'ils règlent à leur choix l'emploi des plus grands cœurs,
Qu'ils ont pour qui les sert des grâces, des faveurs,
Et qu'on n'a jamais droit sur leur reconnaissance.

(2059 ff.)

This is a splendidly written scene; but the speed of the winding up after this (in a pair of scenes of only fifty-two lines) is surprising. Aglatide only discovers whom she is to marry five lines before the end.

As an additional novelty Corneille gives us in this play a new kind of ending, largely but by no means entirely 'happy' since it depends on the painful and, one may well say, heroic self-sacrifice of the central figure. But interesting and intelligent as it is, it is followed by no other tragedy or *comédie heroïque* that uses *vers libres*.

Attila: a parody?

There is clearly one feature that links *Tite* and *Agésilas* with *Attila*, which was produced in the long interval that separates them – the love that a ruler has to sacrifice for reasons of state. But in the first and last we take it seriously, and in *Attila* we cannot, for the ruler, an ugly despot, makes himself ridiculous, and his motives turn out to be simply the chances of personal aggrandizement.

But how is one to write about a work one does not understand? How, to begin with, could Corneille – who knew better – have perpetrated that undignified denouement by haemorrhage? – not a nosebleed, it is true (though the sources say it was),[3] but something worse and messier, after a blockage of the nose (which Corneille dextrously avoids naming)?

Sa rage qui renaît en même temps le tue.
L'impétueuse ardeur de ces transports nouveaux
A son sang prisonnier ouvre tous les canaux;
Son élancement perce ou rompt toutes les veines,
Et ces canaux ouverts sont autant de fontaines
Par o l'âme et le sang se pressent de sortir
Pour terminer sa rage et nous en garantir.
Sa vie à longs ruisseaux se répand sur le sable.

(1754 ff.)

A horrifying ending – which is worth quoting in case some readers may have missed it – brilliantly kept just within the widest limits of *bienséance*, which suddenly winds up an action in which the wicked ogre has been tormenting all his victims at will, till he is whipped away 'pour accommoder toutes choses, sur le point que les acteurs ne savent plus comment les terminer' (I cite the theorist of the *Discours*[4] against the poet of *Attila*; it is almost a prophetic self-condemnation). Critics talk nowadays about Providentialism, as if political or historical meditation had strengthened Corneille's faith in divine intervention. In this country we prefer to invoke the concept of Poetic Justice, where the good end happily, and the bad unhappily – that is what

Fiction means, as Miss Prism has taught us. Our poet has been quite candid about his reasons:

> Nous ne saurions voir un honnête homme sur notre théâtre sans lui souhaiter la prospérité, et nous fâcher de ses infortunes. Cela fait que quand il en demeure accablé, nous sortons avec chagrin, et remportons une espèce d'indignation contre l'auteur et les acteurs.[5]

And who would wish to incur that?

This, perhaps pedantic, theoretical objection is not all. One cannot defend oneself from a certain uneasiness – which some critics, captivated by the study of Corneille's political thought, do not seem to feel – at the mixture of a make-believe world of cruel ogres and captive princesses with that of would-be serious political activity; we have noted a somewhat similar mixture in *Agésilas*, but here the very motives and plans of the schemers seem to be contaminated with motives of romantic comedy and fail to carry conviction. We can recognize – is it parody? – a King who plans, unsuccessfully, like Sertorius, to sacrifice Love to Policy; but there is not a tinge of tragedy in the whole action.

The play opens with a bullying and contemptuous summons to two captive kings, 'nos deux rois', whom Attila forces to act as his counsellors, only to scold them for failing to agree (265 ff.). They produce an analysis, which has been praised, of the balance of power in Europe, with the (Eastern) Roman Empire in decline and Frankish force promising to rise (which occasions prophetic eulogies of France). Attila has demanded, simultaneously, the hand of a princess from each:

> L'une sera ma femme et l'autre mon otage.
> Si j'offense par là l'un des deux souverains,
> Il craindra pour sa sœur, qui reste entre mes mains
>
> (62–4)

But which one is it expedient to marry? he wishes to know. We discover soon after that each of the two Kings has only been finding arguments to preserve from the Hun's clutches the princess he has fallen in love with. A parody of a conference-scene then? No, for that duplicity of motive was true of Cinna and Maxime, and *Cinna* seems quite serious: it is the mechanical simplicity of the motivation that seems at fault.

The princesses arrive (Act II). They are, of course, indignant at their treatment and determined to uphold their *gloire* each in her different way. Honorie, the Roman (or Byzantine) is full of her dignity, and ends by *tutoyer* Attila. Ildione is determined, if she has to marry the King, to murder him on his marriage-bed (699 ff.) – a plan which went against the moral sense of the time (Corneille's time). The marriage vows imposed more onerous burdens than the obvious one, according to the casuistry of *la gloire*: Quinault's Scythian queen Tomiris must avenge the death of a man who forced her to marry him, even on the lover who nearly rescued her in time:

> Pour venger un mari, commence ici de croire
> Qu'il suffit, sans l'aimer, que l'on aime la gloire;
> C'est mon époux haï qu'on a percé de coups;
> Mais, tout haï qu'il est, c'est toujours mon époux.
>
> (*La mort de Cyrus*, V. 2)

Just so, Racine's Andromaque knows she would lose the right to hate Pyrrhus if he forced her to marry him – 'Tous mes ressentments lui seraient asservis' (*Andromaque*, 1011).[6]

Attila has barely met Ildione when he decides that she is not politically the proper match for him; but he finds himself so madly in love with her that he begs her to refuse him.

> Je veux, je tâche en vain d'éviter par la fuite
> Ce charme dominant qui marche à votre suite.
>
> (821–2)

This is the man whom Corneille wishes us to accept as a *fin politique*. 'Un héros ivre qui se veut faire har de sa maîtresse de gaîté de coeur', said Racine, maliciously, and falsely as to every detail, but not so unjustly at bottom; for this is parody of the great Cornelian theme of renunciation of love for reasons of policy. Ildione obliges him; – but why does she deliberately provoke Honorie by handing her Attila as her leavings? 'Il était tout à moi . . . Je vous en fais un don' (939–41). Not, surely, as a spiteful act of triumph such as Corneille too often allows his heroines; for Honorie is no rival, though her airs may have sorely provoked the less distinguished princess; the words are presumably in order to insult Attila, who hears them.

The barbarian King has been touched and amazed at Ildione's professed love:

Quoi! vous pourriez m'aimer, Madame, à votre tour?
Qui sème tant d'horreurs fait naître peu d'amour.
Qu'aimeriez-vous en moi? Je suis cruel, barbare,
Je n'ai que ma fierté, que ma fureur de rare.
On me craint, on me hait, on me nomme en tout lieu
La terreur des mortels et le fléau de Dieu.

(879–84)

Souvenez-vous enfin que je suis Attila,
Et que c'est dire tout que d'aller jusque-là.

(891 ff.)

With the other characters however he remembers to be a barbarian and shows – or rather Corneille shows – a certain virtuosity in reconciling his tyrannous harshness with the decorous modes of speech of tragedy.

Si nous nous emportons, j'irai plus loin que vous,
Madame.
Honorie Les grands cœurs parlent avec franchise.
Attila Quand je m'en souviendrai, n'en soyez pas surprise,
Et si je vous épouse avec ce souvenir,
Vous voyez le passé, jugez de l'avenir.
Je vous laisse y penser. Adieu, Madame.

(1068–73)

How direct and muscular this verse can be! Corneille must have remembered his comedies; or the exercise of *vers libres* may have done him good.

There are reminiscences of the wicked Cléopâtre (from *Rodogune*) when Attila balances threats and promises, to gratify the audience's taste for symmetries of plot: Honorie must choose marriage with himself or his captain of guards Octar 'dans une heure' (1236). One vassal king, and finally both, are egged on to kill the other for the reward of his mistress's hand (IV. 4, V. 3).

I have said I do not understand this play because I thought Corneille had made himself incapable of committing these blunders – blunders as they appear to me, and as I should have expected them to appear to him. So I have no alternative but to set it aside, with *Théodore* (p. 46), as a failure of my personal powers of interpretation. Corneille must have chosen on an impulse to try an unexplored path, then let himself be blinded to its disadvantages. He lost his throw: 'on n'est pas toujours heureux'.[7] Or perhaps we cannot even say that, for *Attila* had quite a respectable success – the last in the poet's career.

The two *Bérénices*

There seems no reason to doubt that the duel of the two *Bérénices* of Corneille and Racine was a deliberate contest of the type which was frequently seen in the mid-seventeenth century; though the romantic legend of Henriette d'Angleterre's secret intervention has been dropped. There is another reason to doubt it besides those with which we are familiar: if Corneille had known that a royal patroness expected some sentimental allusions to her own (or Marie Mancini's) parting with the King, he could not have made a worse job of it – the monarch he depicts is vacillating and irresolute to a point that would be ignominious were it not so pathetic; he needs the assistance of his mistress to conquer his passion for her. Pathetic it is; we will not say tragic, nor will Corneille, who calls his play a *comédie héroïque*. Racine *will* claim the title tragedy for his quite different rendering of the subject, even though the brilliant and famous definition he offers of the genre introduces certain equivocal expressions:

> Il suffit *que l'action en soit grande, que les acteurs en soient héroïques*, que les passions y soient excitées, et que tout s'y ressente de cette tristesse majestueuse qui fait tout le plaisir de la tragédie. (Preface: my italics.)

It seems likely that Racine was the aggressor, or rather that he chose to take up the (unintended) challenge of a subject chosen by his rival; for it is a typical 'matrimonial' subject dealing with love renounced for political reasons and one of a long line that will only end with *Pulchérie*, whereas Racine had never chosen such a subject, and never would again.

Racine claimed to have been drawn to the subject by its extreme simplicity, reminiscent of the ancient taste. He was in fact taking up a charge made by d'Aubignac nine years before – that all expression of emotion was being 'étouffée' in Corneille's recent plays by an excess of material. Racine had been unjust in his previous preface (to *Britannicus*) in complaining of 'une multitude de choses qui pourraient à peune arriver en plusieurs semaines' – it is not events that abound in Corneille's plays of this period, but schemes, ambitions, hopes and fears entertained by the various characters. Thus, the story of Bérénice is in Suetonius that of a simple reluctant parting of lovers, and Racine will add little to the necessary exposition of historical background (the siege of Jerusalem); the middle will be filled with the remorse of his Titus – the only lover in seventeenth-century drama, I fancy, who cares how his mistress will take the end of their love – his two failures to convey his intentions, and the seemingly irrelevant secret love of Antiochus, which in fact is indispensable to bring about the parting. Hence the austerely sombre elegiac tone which is the great beauty of the play.

Corneille must have foreseen a huge empty middle section, and contrived for it the usual invented complication with which he opens the play (as he had in *Oedipe*).

Domitia and Domitian are genuine historical figures, though without any connection with Berenice. The former made herself a danger to the state by asserting rights to the throne derived from her father, a failed candidate for the empire, and from Nero, a collateral of hers. Vespasian had wished to avert the danger by marrying her to his son Tite (to adopt the more French form of the name used by Corneille); but already she had attracted the love of Tite's brother Domitian, as the best available step towards her ambition, and they had become in love with one another. Now, in the first scene of the play, we find her parading her grief at being 'forced' to sacrifice this love to the throne. She is a baffling puzzle for the modern reader: Corneille's parody of the male heroes he had sometimes used? She refuses to be cornered by the two men (II.3) and refuses to confess her real preference; and she imperiously demands of Domitian the obedient service of a lover to help her to obtain his rival (1175 ff.). This is patently ridiculous, and nobody takes her political claims seriously either, unless it is Domitian. And yet we may remember Don Alvar obliged by his *gloire* to desert Doña Elvira for a chance of the throne of Castille (*Don Sanche*, III, 1). Let us simply suppose that Corneille constructed the character to fit the role required, and developed it with some gusto. She is a real danger: we shall find her in a moment of anger, talking of suborning assassins against Tite: 'Je ne suis pas à vous [Domitian], je suis à qui me venge' (1204).

Her lover Domitian has splendidly uncomplicated sentiments, though his methods are devious: he only wants to get her, whether she likes it or not – a fitting text for the much-quoted homily that his confidant Albin preaches on the essentially self-regarding nature of love:

> Seigneur, s'il m'est permis de parler librement,
> Dans toute la nature aime-t-on autrement?
> L'amour propre est la source en nous de tous les autres:
> C'en est le sentiment qui forme tous les nôtres.

Lui seul allume, éteint, ou change nos désirs:
Les objets de nos vœux le sont de nos plaisirs.
Vous-même, qui brûlez d'une ardeur si fidèle,
Aimez-vous Domitie, ou vos plaisirs en elle,
Et quand vous aspirez à des liens si doux,
Est-ce pour l'amour d'elle, ou pour l'amour de vous?

. . . .

Et vous n'aimez que vous, quand vous croyez l'aimer.

(277 ff.)

Tite's father has died, leaving him a free man; but he has let himself be contracted to marry Domitie – the date is four days distant – and he wonders if he can do it:

En vain de mon hymen Rome presse la pompe
J'y veux de la lenteur, j'aime qu'on l'interrompe,
Et n'ose résister aux dangereux souhaits
De préparer toujours et n'achever jamais. (411 ff.)

In vain he is reminded that on accepted political principles 'En un mot, il vous faut la perdre ou l'épouser' (426); he cannot bring himself to take the violent alternative.

But at this point Albin, acting without orders but in his master's interests, to gain a day (and save the Unity of Time) brings Bérénice back to Rome. Tite's dismay is comic, and he escapes with all haste:

Je sais votre zèle, et l'admire,
Madame, et pour me voir possesseur de l'Empire,
Pour me rendre vos soins, je ne méritais pas
Que rien vous pût résoudre à quitter vos Etats,
Qu'une si grande Reine en formât la pensée.
Un voyage si long vous doit avoir lassée:
Conduisez-la, mon frère, en son appartement; (636 ff.)

and from now on begins the series of moves and countermoves that fills the middle of this play.

Domitian offers himself to Bérénice, to arouse Tite's jealousy and make it more certain that he will relinquish Domitie (III. I); alternatively, later, he asks his brother to let him marry Bérénice in compensation for Domitie (IV. 5). He works hard lobbying the Senators in Bérénice's interest, expecting to see Tite jump at the chance of marrying her if it is offered to him. Tite is firm enough in putting off Domitie's demands and refusing her to his brother; but ignominously weak before Bérénice, actually offering to abdicate and go away with her – 'Et soit de Rome esclave et maître qui voudra.' (1034) – doing nothing in fact over the great decision except refusing to make it yet. He is about to dissolve the Senate which is likely to vote on its attitude (1659 ff.) when news comes that it has divided. Domitian has done his work so well that it approves Tite's choice and 'adopts' Bérénice as a Roman to remove that obstacle to her ascent of the throne.

Now comes the paradoxical twist that Corneille has reserved for his denouement: the Queen, her *gloire* abundantly satisfied, can find the *générosité* to understand Tite's position and refuse to marry him.

Tite will remain in power. He will not marry Domitie or any other; Domitian will take her and inherit the throne (as historically he did) so Domitie must be content with that. We do not see her receive the decision, and must imagine the scene.

The ending is presented as a glorious triumph of heroic renunciation: it is neither 'happy' nor 'unhappy' – the 'problem' has been solved, but Tite foregoes the only thing he wanted, and only Domitian gets what he wanted; but we are not sure that it is a good thing (and history says that he divorced Domitie later).

Between *Tite et Bérénice* and *Pulchérie*, Corneille paused to join Molière and Quinault in composing the machine play, *Psyché*; but we need not stop to consider this. It was an assignment, and proved only Corneille's adaptability, speed in working and skill in versifying.

Pulchérie: a coda

This Tragedy (why not *comédie heroïque*? no one dies, or looks like dying, and the denouement is the cancellation of a marriage that has no historical foundation) is hard to see as not meant to be the end of a series – the 'matrimonial' series, or perhaps, if Corneille was feeling ill and depressed, the end of a life-work. It takes over from *Agésilas* and *Tite* the theme of the heroically-willed renunciation of a love-match, but many of the features have been reduced in importance and as it were eroded: there is no foreign queen, marriage with whom might lead to civil commotion; and one feature is inverted: the monarch who has to renounce is an empress, and she makes the decision, paradoxically as before in *Tite*, just at the moment when opposition has almost ceased; the obstacle is simply the fact that her affianced bridegroom Léon (a historical personage and a subsequent emperor, but for whom Pulchérie never in history had this attachment) is just too young to have impressed anybody but herself as a fit candidate for the Empire as her consort. What history says of her age (she was fifty-one) should be forgotten, as unfortunately A. Stegmann has not forgotten it, because it makes nonsense of her relation with Léon, and particularly his with her.

There is less action in this play than in any other Corneille wrote: two votes of the Senate are awaited with suspense, then announced (II. 1; V. 2); by the first, Pulchérie is created empress in her own right, the second concerns the marriage she should make. The long interval is filled with talk – justifications, explanations, expostulations, plotting of political moves. The Dramatis Personae have been reduced: beside the empress there are four characters – Léon's sister and ally Irène, betrothed to Aspar who will marry her or not according as she seems likely to further his ambitions; the faithful old statesman and soldier Martian who tries to hide his unseasonable love from Pulchérie, and his daughter Justine. There are, remarkably enough, no confidants, though the two women (both unhistorical) to some extent act in this role with the empress.

She is daughter of the Emperor of the East, now dead, and elder sister of Théodose II, a feeble-minded prince whom she has forced to let her rule through him. Now that he has died and 'l'Empire est à donner'; she wants it for herself, but of course in a man's world there must be a husband to enforce respect (and to father heirs – inheritance being, as always for Corneille, the only guarantee of political stability): Théodose has been useless, but better than nothing: 'Estimé d'assez peu, mais obéi de tous' (1204). Léon had hoped, and so had she, that she could induce the Senate to make him emperor, so that then he could marry her. But in view of the doubts she has been expressing about his eligibility, Léon, on his sister's advice, has been just too clever and engineered a vote in favour of Pulchérie herself. And now, the choice of a husband engages her responsibility (and her *gloire* in the not impossible case of the choice being overruled) (962 ff.): 'Je suis impératrice, et j'étais Pulchérie' (754, cf 793 ff.). Had the Senate made itself responsible for what she thought the right choice, but an unpopular one, she could joyfully have fallen in with it. Corneille leaves no doubt as to the reality of her love – like that of Agésilas or Tite it must be shown as real to be the object of a heroic renunciation:

> Léon seul est ma joie, il est mon seul désir,
> Je n'en puis choisir d'autre, et n'ose le choisir:

Depuis trois ans unie à cette chère idée,
J'en ai l'âme à toute heure, en tous lieux, obsédée,
Rien n'en détachera mon cœur que le trépas.

(847 ff.)

Not that she had not recognized her opposing desire for power:

Trône qui m'éblouis, titres qui me flattez,
Pourrez-vous me valoir ce que vous me coûtez?

(855 ff.)

and done her best, in the initial scene of the play, to display her sentiment as a passionless affection such as a prudent ruler could avow:

Je vous aime, Léon, et n'en fais point mystère:
Des feux tels que les miens n'ont rien qu'il faille taire.
Je vous aime, et non point de cette folle ardeur
Que les yeux éblouis font maîtresse du cœur,
Non d'un amour conçu par les sens en tumulte,
A qui l'âme applaudit sans qu'elle se consulte,
Et qui ne concevant que d'aveugles désirs,
Languit dans les faveurs, et meurt dans les plaisirs.
Ma passion pour vous, généreuse et solide,
A la vertu pour âme, et la raison pour guide,
La gloire pour objet . . . (1ff.)

But Corneille takes pleasure in painting the complexity of her motives and emotions: as the final vote approaches she discovers with some horror that she is perhaps more empress than lover:

Justine, plus j'y pénse, et plus je m'inquiète:
Je crains de n'avoir plus une amour si parfaite,
Et que si de Léon on me fait un époux,
Un bien si désiré ne me soit plus si doux.
Je ne sais si le rang m'aurait fait changer d'âme,
Mais je tremble à penser que je serais sa femme . . .

(1437 ff.)

The vote is at last announced (III. 2): the Senate refuses to designate a husband and leaves Pulchérie free to make her own choice, which is just what she desired least: 'Il pouvait le choisir' (1469).

So she makes her choice, deliberately painful and deliberately paradoxical, refusing (like Bérénice) the option that had become quite easy to take, and was in fact expected by public opinion. It is heroic, as in the earlier plays, if one is willing to take it as such, but it is the only event that takes the place of what would have been the denouement of a tragedy.

There is plenty of time (after V. 2) to settle the fate of Léon and everybody else. The slow unfolding of the empress's decisions (unlike the hurried matches of *Agésilas*) keeps up the element of surprise:

> Ne partez pas, Seigneur, je les tromperai tous,
> Et puisque de ce choix aucun ne me dispense,
> Il est fait, et de tel à qui pas un ne pense.
>
> (1516 ff.)

She bestows her hand – but only her hand, to keep her promise to Léon that no other should have her 'personne' – on the 'vieil et cassé' Martian, and Léon on Justine who had recently fallen in love with him while executing Pulchérie's errands; the scene (II.2) in which the girl confesses this to her father, in return for his confession of his autumnal love, is a beautiful scene of sentimental comedy which relieves and varies the prevailing tone of intrigue. Léon protests, but is coaxed into the scheme Pulchérie had formed (but which before her full renunciation she could hardly bear to contemplate, 1173 ff.). Aspar receives his due, for having been unashamedly ready to try to marry whichever, of Irène or Justine, could make him son-in-law or brother-in-law of the new Emperor-Consort. He is to keep his former promise to marry Irène in two days – an unwelcome match to her, one might think, but she will be free to reject him, after making good the damage to her *gloire* of his long delay (1251).

So there is ambiguity in the colours with which Corneille paints both the contending values of heroic Policy and Love. *Raison d'Etat* is tainted with love of power. Love, though it hinders heroic (or political) action and is put aside firmly by the heroine, is not solely the heedless self-seeking that we see in Léon, as earlier in Domitian (though Léon does have the grace to let his 'rage inquiète' be melted by Pulchérie's evident distress, 1637 ff.): it wears gentler and tenderer lineaments in Justine and Martian.

Suréna: a palinode?

Corneille ends his career with what must be called a palinode – not merely because of the preponderant place which, at last, he allows to the love interest, but even more because with a characteristic somersault he upsets the scale of values to which he had accustomed us. Love is, or may be, too strong to be resisted and need therefore not be concealed from its object – we rub our eyes, but that is what he makes his heroine say:

> L'amour dès qu'il le veut, se fait un privilège,
> Et quand de se forcer ses désirs sont lassés,
> Lui-même à n'en rien taire il s'enhardit assez.
>
> (146 ff.)

and in *Suréna* the rejected bridegroom in the political marriage and his father the King are presented as cruel tyrants.

Orode King of Parthia has survived a simultaneous threat from Rome and Armenia. His general Suréna has routed the Romans under Crassus, and he himself has intimidated Armenia (which in negotiations had inclined to the side of Rome) into signing a peace and sending the Armenian princess Eurydice to Séleucie to marry the Parthian King's son. But Eurydice has fallen victim to that accident which *l'Infante* in *Le Cid* had known it was her duty to avoid, the accident which Monime, in Racine's recent *Mithridate*, had thanked the Gods for helping her to escape (*Mith.* 409). She had met Suréna who had gone to Arménie as emissary of his country for the negotiations, and the two had fallen in love: an exchange of glances, an unguarded word, had done the trick:

> L'amour s'en mêla même, et tout son entretien
> Sembla m'offrir son cœur, et demander le mien.
> Il l'obtint, et mes yeux, que charmait sa présence,
> Soudain avec les siens en firent confidence. (47 ff.)
>
> Un accord imprévu confondait nos soupirs,
> Et d'un mot échappé la douceur hasardée
> Trouvait l'âme en tous deux toute persuadée. (56 ff.)

Eurydice fills the whole first act of exposition with her sad plight. To an earlier generation of heroines in other plays it would have appeared quite scandalous, especially the openness with which she talks about it to her confidant, to Suréna's sister, and Suréna himself.

She has nothing to fear in Parthia, as the daughter of a foreign monarch, though her father may have something to say when she returns. But she rarely mentions him, and it is her version of the story that he will receive. She insists that she means to honour the engagement she has been forced into; she had hoped to be able to stifle her feelings once Suréna had been lost to sight: but here is Suréna, in Séleucie, waiting to grace the wedding with his presence.

All she wants to do now is to stall – she is one of the many Cornelian characters (un-Cornelian in the other sense) who temporize to postpone the painful act or decision they know they will have to make. She can only think of prolonging the agony and the ecstasy of her love, and thinks little of the feelings of her lover, except that he must not die.

Vivez, Seigneur, vivez, afin que je languisse, (261)
. . .
Je veux qu'un noir chagrin à pas lents me consume,
Qu'il me fasse à longs traits goûter son amertume,
Je veux, sans que la mort ose me secourir,
Toujours aimer, toujours souffrir, toujours mourir.
(265–68)

The prospect appals Suréna who says he wants only to die at once; but he is a submissive lover according to the rules – or, if they seem too strange, inhuman and unreal, we can I think decode them here, and say that he is anxious to spare his mistress additional pain.

But how can she delay the inevitable marriage? She is ingenious enough to pick a quarrel with her betrothed, Pacorus – there is no other possible interpretation. She forces him to notice the frigidity of her reception of him, offering him her hand without her heart (496 ff.). He has what we might consider the delicacy to inquire about 'Quelque autre amour plus fort' (511); but, as we have seen, this is indelicacy (p. 99), and it calls forth a resounding rebuke.

Ah! ce n'est point pour moi que je rougis de honte.
Si j'ai pu faire un choix, je l'ai fait assez beau
Pour m'en faire un honneur jusque dans le tombeau,
Et quand je l'avouerai, vous aurez lieu de croire
Que tout mon avenir en aimera la gloire.
Je rougis, mais pour vous, qui m'osez demander
Ce qu'on doit avoir peine à se persuader,
Et je ne comprends point avec quelle prudence
Vous voulez qu'avec vous j'en fasse confidence,
Vous qui près d'un hymen accepté par devoir,
Devriez sur ce point craindre de trop savoir.
(522 ff.)

Corneille may have remembered Racine's Monime here, in the *Mithridate* of some months ago. Monime, alone and unsupported, refuses to marry Mithridate for what is in fact quite a different reason:

Mithridate knows she has another love, but he has used an ignoble trick to obtain an avowal:

> Et le tombeau, Seigneur, est moins triste pour moi
> Que le lit d'un époux qui m'a fait cet outrage,
> Qui s'est acquis sur moi ce cruel avantage,
> Et qui me préparant un éternel ennui,
> M'a fait rougir d'un feu qui n'était pas pour lui.
>
> (*Mith.* 1350 ff.)

and the tomb it would have been, but for a fifth-act *coup de théâtre.*

Two different considerations of matrimonial policy threaten Corneille's pair of lovers, creating what is perhaps a disturbance of the unity of action: Suréna is not merely the undeclared rival of Pacorus: he is yet another case of the vassal who has become a menace to his suzerain; indeed A. Stegmann tells us that the historical Surena is a *locus classicus* for the Machiavellian treatment of such a figure in sixteenth-century Italian political writings,[8] and it is no doubt there that Corneille found him, and tacked his sad fate onto the invented romance of Eurydice.

> La saine politique a deux extrémités.
> Quoi qu'ait fait Suréna, quoi qu'il en faille attendre,
> Ou faites-le périr, ou faites-en un gendre.
> Puissant par sa fortune, et plus par son emploi,
> S'il devient par l'hymen l'appui d'un autre Roi,
> Si dans les différends que le ciel vous peut faire,
> Une femme l'entraîne au parti de son père.
> Que vous servira lors, Seigneur, d'en murmurer?
> Il faut, il faut le perdre, ou vous en assurer:
> Il n'est point de milieu.
>
> (727 ff.)

Not a word has been spoken of the marriage into which Suréna is to be forced; but it is known that Orode's daughter Mandane is expected to appear in Séleucie, and Eurydice quickly suspects that it will be for that purpose. (Mandane has been the name of a Persian character in *Agésilas*; but Corneille clearly could not put himself to the trouble of finding another Parthian name; and this character never appears on the stage. Why, for that matter, is the Armenian Eurydice's name Greek?). In her first scene with Suréna Eurydice pleads:

N'épousez point Mandane: exprès on l'a mandée,
. . .
N'ajoutez point, Seigneur, à des malheurs si grands
Celui de vous unir au sang de mes tyrans,
De remettre en leurs mains le seul bien qui me reste,
Votre coeur: un tel don me serait trop funeste,
Je veux qu'il me demeure, et malgré votre Roi,
Disposer d'une main qui ne peut être à moi.
. . .
Il faut qu'un autre hymen me mette en assurance,
N'y portez, s'il se peut, que de l'indifférence,
Mais par de nouveaux feux dussiez-vous me trahir,
Je veux que vous aimiez afin de m'obéir.
Je veux que ce grand choix soit mon dernier ouvrage,
Qu'il tienne lieu vers moi d'un éternel hommage.

(277 ff., 321 ff.)

He must have descendants, and so must marry somebody; but he must let her give him away to some other bride.

This strange-seeming desire, which we have seen before, is a product of jealousy; Eurydice admits it (98). The savagely possessive Sophonisbe, when she had lost Massinisse, had wanted him to marry a sister-in-law, and reacted furiously when he seemed about to honour his engagement to Eryxe (p. 93f.). Domitie would not hear of Domitian marrying Bérénice (*Tite et Bérénice*, 1279 ff; cf. 1283 ff); and even Bérénice has the same reaction:

Seigneur, faites-moi grâce: épousez Sulpitie,
Ou Camille, ou Sabine, et non pas Domitie;
Choisissez-en quelqu'une enfin dont le bonheur
Ne m'ôte que la main, et me laisse le cœur.

(ibid. 971 ff.)

This is natural, no doubt, and pathetic. But what are we to say of Eurydice when it becomes clear that her lover's life depends on his marrying the rival (unless Eurydice placates Orode by celebrating her own marriage, which she will not)? We remember Plautine pushing Othon into another match which would save his life (and hers), and resolutely contemplating an utterly abhorrent marriage herself to save him (*Othon*, I. 2, IV. 1). So Corneille *is* capable of conceiving heroines able to make these sacrifices: this heroine of his is not.

The situation can hardly be called complicated; the action is not so at all. In one sense indeed, there is none. J. Scherer[9] has pointed out the great simplicity, dramatically, of this play, which has only eighteen scenes, the lowest number of any five-act play of its time – which means few comings and goings (characters enter as required, with little regard to the stipulation that Corneille once thought important, that one should know why they come, and the motive should be acceptable:[10] they are obviously in the green-room awaiting their call), no new initiatives, no reversals, no hopes raised or disappointed. The lovers are quite early suspected, and each is put under pressure which they fight with the best arguments they can muster. Eurydice continues to find reasons why she cannot marry Pacorus, at least forthwith. She and Suréna urge, with much dexterity and diplomatic disguise, that Orode and Pacorus simply cannot afford to dispense with the great defender of Parthia. Suréna claims that Mandane must not marry beneath her, and that his sister Palmis could marry Pacorus and provide the link with the royal family (933 ff.). Corneille has built up an ingenious sub-plot, according to which Palmis has been loved by Pacorus, and jilted for Eurydice, but he is not able to make much use of this invention.

The royal patience wears thin. Veiled threats (957, 1053) give place to acts – guards are posted round the palace (1074)– and threats less veiled. Eurydice loses her ill-founded confidence that 'on n'oserait' to attack Suréna; but for all her alarm she cannot bring herself to accept Pacorus (1136) nor to contemplate Suréna's marriage with Mandane. He must do it without her knowledge – but of course he won't (1143 ff.).

After an angry scene (V. 4) in which Suréna almost confesses to Pacorus that he had loved Eurydice before him, Orode makes himself clear to Eurydice – Suréna is to be 'exiled' to some country place of his, on the pretext that his refusal of Mandane might give rise to violence from the royal family (1470 ff.).

He issues his ultimatum:

> Il me faut un hymen: choisissez l'un ou l'autre,
> Ou lui dites adieu pour le moins jusqu'au vôtre.
>
> (1497 ff.)

The last meeting of the lovers (V. 2–3) is an emotional climax. Suréna makes his farewell as he goes to his 'exile'. Eurydice speaks of the one marriage demanded of him; he attributes their parting not to this (perhaps to exculpate Eurydice?) but to his excessive services:

Mon crime véritable est d'avoir aujourd'hui
Plus de nom que mon Roi, plus de vertu que lui,
Et c'est de là que part cette secrète haine
Que le temps ne rendra que plus forte et plus pleine.

(1511–14)

He hopes to die soon; she thinks only of putting off the evil day:

. . . l'unique bonheur que j'y puis espérer,
C'est de toujours promettre et toujours différer.

(1559 ff.)

Palmis, who comes to say goodbye, is clear-sighted about the danger, now a virtual certainty, of assassination. If he would only take the 'asile' offered, the hand of Mandane! She turns to Eurydice when he proves obdurately faithful to her will.

P. Mais vous ne m'aidez point à le persuader,
Vous qui d'un seul regard pourriez tout décider?
Madame, ses périls ont-ils de quoi vous plaire?
E. Je crois faire beaucoup, Madame, de me taire,
Et tandis qu'à mes yeux vous donnez tout mon bien,
C'est tout ce que je puis que de ne dire rien.
Forcez-le, s'il se peut, au nœud que je déteste,
Je vous laisse en parler, dispensez-moi du reste.

(1627–34)

The doomed hero makes light of the safety to be gained by that marriage, and tries at last to encourage the women by pooh-poohing the danger. The sister's last appeal is brushed aside.

P. Par toute l'amitié que le sang doit attendre,
Par tout ce que l'amour a pour vous de plus tendre . . .
S. Latendresse n'est point de l'amour d'un héros:
Il est honteux pour lui d'écouter des sanglots,
Et parmi la douceur des plus illustres flammes,
Un peu de dureté sied bien aux grandes âmes.
P. Quoi? vous pourriez . . .
S. Adieu, le trouble où je vous voi
Me fait vous craindre plus que je ne crains le Roi.

(1673–80)

He had treated Eurydice in the same way, asking to be allowed to preserve

cette fermeté
Qui fait de tels jaloux, et qui m'a tant coûté.

(1575–6)

But this is not stoical insensibility, as some critics seem to have thought, but the same retreat as we saw Horace make to protect his resolution which he felt endangered:

Tu me viens de réduire en un étrange point;
Aime assez ton mari pour n'en triompher point,
Va-t'en, et ne rends plus la victoire douteuse,
La dispute déjà m'en est assez honteuse,
Souffre qu'avec honneur je termine mes jours.

(*Horace*, 673 ff.)

The resolve Suréna wishes to keep is simply to give his life to please his mistress. At last Palmis prevails over Eurydice to release him, but after her brother has gone, and too late to do more than create a last-minute suspense.

The ending is stark and bleak – not that much can be made of a death by assassination in a classical tragedy. The news is told in five lines; three arrows from an unknown hand strike the great soldier in the public street. Palmis is distraught, Eurydice as if stunned:

P. Quoi! vous causez sa perte, et n'avez point de pleurs!
E. Non, je ne pleure point, Madame, mais je meurs.
Ormène, soutiens-moi.

(1731 f.)

Does she die on the spot? Corneille omits to tell us; the confidant hopes not. Palmis ends the play with some wild words about vengeance, of which there seems little hope.

So end these martyrs of love, these rebels against *raison d'Etat*. Corneille has indeed 'changed the signs', and ended his career, as everyone has noticed, by holding the rebels up for pity and approval. But let us look at the kind of love it is – it has made Eurydice responsible for her lover's death no less surely than the politic Orode or the jealous Pacorus. We may well be astonished at the conclusion. And yet it seems impossible to doubt that Corneille meant it: he has used Palmis to make the point plain. The pathetic ending has forced us to distinguish, under the red petals of the rose of love, the snake of self-love nestling in its shadow. Perhaps he knew what he was doing, and realized that in this kind of passion, which he had never used before in such a way, he had found a love that is truly tragic.

VII

Corneille's Ideas on Tragedy

I suggested earlier that when he invented that 'French classical tragedy' which was to flourish so proudly for two centuries, Corneille owed less to his competitors than to his own trial and error – or trial and success – and, in some degree, to a variety of other dramatic traditions, and even to Seneca and Aristotle's *Poetics*, which he felt obliged to study. Aristotle furnishes the whole table of contents of his *Discours* on dramatic questions, and he writes with a weary sigh to his literary friend de Pure:

> Je crois qu'après cela il n'y a plus guère de question d'importance à remuer, et que ce qui reste n'est que la broderie qu'y peuvent ajouter la rhétorique, la morale et la politique.[1]

There is one question unanswered that we should have dearly liked to put to him: the question so much debated in our day, which loves to philosophize over what it cannot produce – what is Tragedy? The early definitions answered rather the question, 'what is *a* tragedy?' and Corneille very likely could not have answered this one: it would not have occurred to him, for the concept of *le tragique* was not represented in the vocabulary of the time.[2] I shall not attempt to answer for him; I shall drag in no notions of Destiny or the Human Condition (though Montaigne did coin the phrase). That way lies danger: we cannot be just to Corneille if we try him by laws he never knew.

He had at the back of his mind, I fancy, besides the Aristotelian formulas, the notions which Lanson has summarized in the oft-quoted Four Points[3] – Tragedy was 'historique (la légende équivaut à l'histoire) – royale – sanglante' and 'élevée de style'. Corneille himself demonstrated in *Cinna* that it could do without 'du sang et des morts'; for death he substituted the idea of danger ('l'unité de péril' constituting for him the unity of action in Tragedy, cf. p. 65) – if not 'péril de vie', then that which a monarch may dread more, 'de pertes d'Etats ou de bannissement', one that is removed only at the denouement. 'Une action illustre, extraordinaire, sérieuse' in which characters above the common have to face a situation above the common, in that it involves a threat of the gravest measure. How they faced it, was the playwright's own business; he could make them face it as he would, and it becomes obvious as the century wears on (and as Corneille works on) that the form is very accommodating and will take almost any filling (we may think of the novel today).

Corneille had picked up the notion that the heroic (meaning here, I suppose, simply that which transcends normal human limitations) was of the essence of Tragedy.[4] He seems, in the early days of the Tetralogy, to have decided to make the 'péril' an ordeal, a challenge, which a man proves himself a hero by meeting. *Le Cid* and *Horace* had provided him with such plots. The heroic decision (we could call it existential) has to be made unguided: to renounce what is by no means an ignoble motive – often the love of family, or wife, or mistress – in favour of some higher good, and the struggle has to be seen to be painful; but the will must be strong enough to make the choice and carry it through. This is the only place Corneille leaves for pity – unless it is pity for accessory victims.

This account has satisfied many readers and critics, and it is satisfactory until *Polyeucte* has been left behind. After this, it is bewildering to try to pin Corneille down. The heroic choice is very little used; choice is rarely painful. What baffles is that the formula of 'admiration' in *Nicomède* is propounded so late: it fits the Tetralogy at least as well as that drama, but it tends to make us forget or refuse to notice *Rodogune* and *Héraclius*, plays of intellectual puzzle, surprise and suspense.

The 'matrimonial' plays, with their scenario of the dynastic marriage to be endured or avoided, do bring back the theme of the painful choice; but here we are surprised to find its very painfulness accentuated. The reluctant hero becomes an object of pity, or sometimes he fails and becomes for a moment an object of contempt and ridicule. The women characters are able to show more heroism then the male. *Pulchérie* contains a paradoxical refusal to take a course long-desired just at the moment when it becomes easy. *Suréna*, at the close, carries a protest against what we thought was an a priori positive value, the marriage for *raison d'Etat*; it exalts love, and dissects it pitilessly.

And this meagre and unsatisfactory summary is all that a careful study has been able to produce. I need not repeat that I cannot see the poet working his way towards some climax that might crown, and explain, his thinking. I see rather a reflective and resourceful chess-player setting up a series of games with pieces corresponding to the highest interests that he recognizes in the world around him –

changing the values of the pieces at will (is love a snare, or a good for which it is right to sacrifice much?) or even the rules of the game. Is there a lesson? I shall not attempt to suggest one.

But the question may be asked whether we have not here another sign of Corneille's love of disconcerting his public, of which we have seen so many signs – his refusal to repeat a success (a tragedy follows *Le Cid*, *Pertharite* follows *Nicomède*), his apparent desire to shock, to disturb, to surprise more than we know we must expect to be surprised by anything from Corneille. Chimène loyal to her father's murderer was the first case, and perhaps gave Corneille occasion to meditate; there is also Horace turned murderer (this was an unavoidable datum of the story, but nothing forced Corneille to choose that story); Polyeucte giving away a loving wife; Pertharite offering his crown to ransom his; Rodélinde offering to marry a usurper only if he kills her son; Sertorius or Othon failing his test and getting laughed at (pure inventions of Corneille, these failures). Such shocking incidents are I believe deliberately created, and closely linked with the playwright's belief that success depended on the unexpected.

The purpose of Tragedy was to give pleasure (its proper pleasure), Aristotle had said. If a play did that it was applauded, and its success was irrefutable proof of its goodness. 'Mon avis est celui de Térence: puisque nous faisons des poèmes pour être représentés, notre premier but doit être de plaire à la cour et au peuple, et d'attirer un grand monde à leurs représentations' (B 179). He will never appeal against the popular verdict. If *Théodore* had failed, 'Je veux bien ne m'en prendre qu'à ses défauts, et la croire mal faite, puisqu'elle a été mal suivie. J'aurais tort de m'opposer au jugement du public: il m'a été trop avantageux en d'autres ouvrages' (B 127). (This at least is his public attitude; it will not stop him defending the brothel episode in this play.)

But he believed that success depended greatly on the novelty, the unexpectedness, of the work. This must explain the 'zigzag' courses we have remarked on. 'Vous connaissez l'humeur de nos Français; ils aiment la nouveauté; et je hasarde *non tam meliora quam nova*, sur l'espérance de les mieux divertir. C'était l'humeur des Grecs dès le temps d'Eschyle,

Apud quos
Illecebris erat et grata novitate morandus
Spectator . . . (B 195)

There must be affectation in this. Corneille was no *poète crotté* determined to play the mountebank and catch his public by offering what was new rather than what he thought better. We can believe that he saw originality as a sign of intellectual superiority; and we can doubt whether the demand for novelty came more strongly from the public than from the poet himself. But also, the idea is closely related in his mind with his doctrine of *admiration*. 'Je vous connais . . .', says Curiace to Horace,

> Mais cette âpre vertu ne m'était pas connue;
> Comme notre malheur elle est au plus haut point:
> Souffrez que je l'admire . . . (504 ff.)

It was by taking her by surprise that Corneille made Mme de Sévigné 'frissonner'. It was the secret of the Sublime, as Corneille might have read (in Latin, though not yet in French) in the pseudo-Longinus, and as Boileau was to apply it later to Corneille himself:

> Le Sublime . . . ne persuade pas proprement, mais il ravit, il transporte, et produit en nous *une certaine admiration mêlée d'etonnement et de surprise* . . . Quand le Sublime vient à éclater où il faut, il renverse tout comme un foudre.[5]

One of Corneille's sources for the story of *Horace*, Dionysius of Halicarnassus, applied to it a word which would have delighted the poet if he could have read it in Greek – the adjective παραδόξος which means 'paradoxical',[6] but not quite literally 'contrary to logic', rather 'against all probability', what nobody could have expected. Corneille always went for the *événement extraordinaire* (see above p. 61) but also for the unexpected device, procedure, effect. The more outrageously improbable the incident, the better, because the more striking ('le sujet d'une belle tragédie doit n'être pas vraisemblable')[7] – provided only that he could take his public with him. He knew it was never certain that he would, but he seems to have enjoyed taking the risk. The public was for him unpredictable; he watched its reactions, but there is little sign that he ever tried to study its taste. Perhaps this is what Tallemant meant by saying 'Je lui trouve plus de génie que de jugement'.[8]

The shock of novelty, though dangerous, was especially necessary, he thought, in a career as long as his. 'Aussi est-ce la vingt et unième [pièce] que j'ai mise sur le théâtre; et après y avoir fait réciter quarante mille vers, il est bien malaisé de trouver quelque chose de nouveau, sans s'écarter un peu du grand chemin, et se mettre au hasard de s'égarer.' (B 150). (The play thus apologetically presented is *Nicomède*, with its appeal to *admiration* and rejection of pity.)

The danger is real and incalculable, or so he says he thinks; perhaps it is an elegant way of shrugging off failures – or drawing attention to successes.

> Cette licence que j'ai prise [with historical fact this time, in *Héraclius*] l'événement [i.e. my success] l'a assez justifiée . . . mais à parler sans fard, je ne voudrais pas [*sic*] conseiller à personne de la tirer en exemple. C'est beaucoup hasarder, et l'on n'est pas toujours heureux; et dans un dessein de cette nature, ce qu'un bon succès fait passer pour une ingénieuse hardiesse, un mauvais le fait prendre pour une témérité ridicule (B 188).

He courted all kinds of risks, with optimism:

> La manière dont je l'ai traitée [the tragedy of *Agésilas*, in *Vers libres*] n'a point d'exemple . et c'est ce qui me l'a fait choisir . . . On court, à la vérité, quelque risque de s'égarer, et même on s'égare assez souvent, quand on s'écarte du chemin battu; mais on ne s'égare pas toutes les fois qu'on s'en écarte. Quelques-uns en arrivent plus tôt où ils prétendent, et chacun peut hasarder à ses périls' (B 169).

A mind of lofty independence, which enjoyed the taste of danger; a compulsive gambler, whose luck ran out, and, we must add, a good loser.

Notes

ABBREVIATIONS

B	(followed by a page reference) P. Corneille, *Writings on the Theatre*, ed. H.T. Barnwell (Blackwell, Oxford, 1965)
Seuil	Corneille, *Œuvres complètes* ed. A. Stegmann (L'Integrale), Ed. du Seuil, 1963
Héroïsme	*André Stegmann, L'heroïsme Cornélien: genèse et signification* (A. Colin, 1968), t.II, L'Europe intellectuelle et le théâtre, Signification
FS	*French studies*
MLR	*Modern Language Review*
PFSCL	*Papers on French Seventeenth-Century Literature* (Tübingen)
R *St.*	*Romance Studies* (University of Wales)

Books in English are published in London, those in French in Paris, unless otherwise stated.

INTRODUCTION

1. As my friend H.T. Barnwell has well said: '[After René Bray] we have been offered the idea of a Corneille reflecting less the aesthetic preoccupations of his day than contemporary events, personalities, political and moral thought, or expressing an ideology (often anachronistic), or writing successive chapters of his spiritual or sentimental autobiography' – 'Corneille in 1663: the tragedy of "Sophonisbe" ', *PFSCL* XI (1984) No. 21, 577–92, p. 577. But such a Corneille is perhaps easier to write about.
2. Cit. and trad. H.W. Lawton, *Handbook of French Renaissance Dramatic Theory* (1949), pp. 130, 133, 136, 140.
3. See Acknowledgements.

I TOWARDS TRAGEDY

1. Page references to Corneille, *Writings on the Theatre*, ed. H.T. Barnwell (1965) are given in this form throughout this book.

Clitandre: tragicomedy in the rules

2. To J. de Schelandre, *Tyr et Sidon* (1628), in Lawton, op. cit., (pp. 115–27), p. 118.
3. Ibid., p. 117.

Medée: almost a tragedy

4. See H.C. Lancaster, *A History of French Dramatic Literature* (1929–42) I 424 ff; G. Brereton, *French Tragic Drama in the 16th and 17th centuries* (1973), pp. 100 ff.
5. Lancaster, op. cit., I 310 n.
6. See D.A. Watts's ed. of the play (Exeter, 1971), p. vii.
7. Third *Discours*, B 77.
8. The episodic character Aegeus, King of Athens, cf. p. [9].
9. Compare the flight depicted in the frontispiece of the Amsterdam ed. of 1664 in Corneille, *Théâtre complet*, ed. G. Couton (Garnier, 1971) t.I 11th figure (unpaginated), and (microscopically and without attribution) in S. Chevalley, *Album Théâtre classique* (1970), p. 27.
10. 'The Stage Settings of Corneille's Early Plays', *Seventeenth-Century French Studies* VII (1985), 184–97, p. 182.
11. *Héraclius*, Au Lecteur, B 190.
12. In all line references to *Médée*, I quote the numbering of the first ed. (1639) reproduced by A. de Leyssac (Geneva, 1978), followed by that of the definitive ed. reproduced by all other modern texts.
13. Chap. 15 (1454ª36).
14. In his ed. (v n 12), p. 38.
15. *Le sentiment de l'amour dans l'œuvre de Pierre Corneille* (1948), p. 294.
16. First *Discours*, B 14.
17. Lettre 9, *Seuil*, p. 853.
18. Tr. A. Way, in *Euripides* (Loeb Classical Library vol. IV, 1919), p. 167.
19. 'That I should shed my children's, my own offspring's blood? . What sins will the poor boys atone? Their sin is that Jason is their father, and, greater sin, that Medea is their mother. Let them die, they are none of mine; let them be lost – they are my own . . . Why, soul, dost hesitate? Anger puts love to flight, and love, anger. O wrath, yield thee to love.' Tr. F.J. Miller, in *Seneca's Tragedies* (Loeb Classical Library, London and New York), vol. I (1927), pp. 305–7.

II. THE TETRALOGY

1. Corneille, *Horace* (Grant and Cutler, 1981).

Le Cid: heroism with a Spanish swagger

2. Ed. L. Lorenzo (Madrid, 1984). I wish to take the opportunity to thank my friend, J.B. Hall, Senior Lecturer in Spanish at the University College of Swansea, for his generous help in writing this section.
3. *La Veuve*, Examen, B 87.
4. The first reference is to the first ed. (1637) as reproduced by P.H. Nurse (Harrap, 1978); the second to the definitive text.

5. Op. cit., 168 f, 170 f.
6. *Cid* (ed. cit.), pp. 33–62.

Horace: the legacy of tragicomedy

7. *Horace, ou Naissance de l'homme* (1952), pp. 107 ff.
8. Cf. H.C. Ault, 'The Tragic Genius of Corneille', *MLR* XLV (1950), 164–76, pp. 168, 175.

Cinna: tragedy with a happy ending

9. See his *Cinna* (London, 1964), p. 21 n1.
10. *Le péché et la grâce* (Univ. de Toulouse – le Mirail, 1984), pp. 102 ff.
11. See Watts, *Cinna*, p. 27.
12. Op. cit., p. 113.
13. In particular W.H. Barber, 'Patriotism and "Gloire" in Corneille's *Horace*', *MLR* XLVI (1951), pp. 368 ff.
14. Corneille will use a character from his *épisode* to *dénouer* his main action – as Maxime here, by his confession to Auguste; Sévère by his intervention with Félix, which hastens Polyeucte's death; Attale by his rescue of Nicomède.
15. Op. cit., pp. 147, 162.
16. R. Bray, *La formation de la doctrine classique en France* (1927, 1951), p. 324.

Polyeucte: the hero as martyr

17. *Corneille et la dialectique du héros* (Gallimard, n.d.), p. 223.
18. Herland, 'L'imprévisible et l'inexplicable dans la conduite du héros comme ressort tragique chez Corneille' in *Le théâtre tragique*, ed. J. Jacquot (CNRS, 1962), pp. 239–49, 243 ff.
19. *Sentiment de l'amour*, chap. XI, pp. 201 ff.
20. Corneille even makes him express, in private to his confidant, a surprisingly Voltairean opinion about the origins of (pagan!) religious beliefs: it is suppressed in 1660 (v. the variants after line 1434).
21. 'Racine et la poétique du regard', in *L'œil rivant* (1961), p. 90.

III THE PRESSURE FALLS

La Mort de Pompée: a feeble imitation

1. A. Adam, *Histoire de la littérature française au xviie siècle*, I (1948), pp. 215 ff, 524 ff; G. Couton, *Corneille* (1958), pp. 34, 54; J. Maurens, *La tragédie sans tragique* (1966), p. 198.
2. Thus he insists that the true aim of his art is to give pleasure (to the great Cardinal!) whereas the latter's protégés all insisted that it was moral profit. See David Clarke, 'Pierre Corneille's occasional and circumstantial writings relating to Cardinal Richelieu (1631–1642)', *FS*, XLI (1987), No. I, 20–36, p. 25.

3. I am sorry not to share my friend H.T. Barnwell's views, in the commentary of his edition of the play (Oxford, 1971).

Rodogune and *Héraclius*: experiments in plot

4. Last sentence of the *Argument*, *Seuil*, p. 465.

Don Sanche and *Nicomède*: swagger and 'admiration'

5. See my '*Cosroès* and *Nicomède*' in *The French Mind, Studies in honour of G. Rudler*, ed. W. Moore et al. (Oxford, 1952), pp. 53–69.

Pertharite: goodbye to *gloire*

6. 'Le sens de *Pertharite*' in *Mélanges . . . offerts à M.R. Pintard* (Univ. de Strasbourg, 1975), pp. 175–84.
7. This line belongs to a speech edited out of III. 4 in 1660 – though the reconciliation scene (V. 5) retains: 'Rendez-moi Rodélinde, et gardez ma couronne' (1827).

IV CORNEILLE RETURNS

The *Discours*: coming to terms with Aristotle

1. *Corneille: Writings on the Theatre* (Oxford, 1965); and see also his *Corneille and Racine: an old parallel revisited* (Oxford, 1982).
2. P. 132.
3. Cf. my *Racine et la Grèce* (1951, 1975), p. 66.
4. Lettre 19, à l'abbé de Pure, *Seuil*, p. 859 f.
5. Granet's *Recueil de dissertations sur plusieurs tragédies de Corneille et Racine* (1714, reprint New York 1975) does not reproduce this fourth *Dissertation*.

Oedipe: Corneille versus Sophocles

6. Rotrou's *Antigone* (1637) seems to have drawn only on an Italian translation of Sophocles; an *Antigone* by Pader d'Assezan has some interest, but dates from 1686. Apart from these only odd borrowings are recorded in some three plays. *V*. *Racine et la Grèce*, pp. 120–29.
7. *Homère en France au xvii*[e] *siècle* (1970).

V TRAGEDY WITHOUT HEROES: the matrimonial group

1. *Héroïsme*, II 522. I am glad to acknowledge my debt to this critic, though I cannot share his view of Corneille's plays as 'une enquête sur l'héroïsme'.

2. '*Sertorius*, comédie tragique', in *The Classical Tradition in French Literature*, ed. H.T. Barnwell *et al.* (Grant and Cutler, 1977), pp. 61–70, p. 68; see also my 'Sertorius: Quand un Romain soupire', *Humanitas*, ed. R.L. Davis et al., (Belfast, 1985).

Sertorius: quand un Romain soupire

3. *Héroïsme* II 518.
4. 'Mes deux heroïnes ont le même caractère de vouloir épouser par ambition un homme pour qui elles n'ont aucun amour . . . 'Lettre 21, à l'abbé de Pure, *Seuil*, p. 861.
5. *Seconde dissertation* . . ., in Granet, *Recueil* I 245.
6. *Héroïsme* II 523.
7. *Défense du* Sertorius . . ., in Granet, *Recueil* I 295–364, p. 347.
8. 'Corneille', in *French Literature and its Background 2: the 17th century*, ed. J. Cruickshank (Oxford, 1969), pp. 17–23; p. 23.

Othon: the unheroic hero

9. Stegmann, *Seuil*, p. 677 n29; *Héroïsme* II 380, 447, 627; Doubrowski, *Corneille et la dialectique du héros*, pp. 375–78. Cf. my 'Minimal Definition of French Classical Tragedy', *FS*, X (1956), pp. 297 ff, p. 301.
10. *Héroïsme* II 447.
11. *V. Héraclius*, Au Lecteur, B 188.
12. *Commentaires sur Corneille*, t.III (*Complete Works*, 55), Banbury, 1975, p. 919. Vinius himself forestalls Voltaire's objection, 231 ff.
13. *Héroïsme* II 480.
14. *Seuil*, p. 477 n.
15. *Héroïsme*, II 433, 381.
16. Les frères Parfaict, cit. Voltaire, *Commentaires* III 913.
17. P. France, 'Corneille' in J. Cruickshank, op. cit., pp. 30–31; Doubrowski, *Corneille*, p. 361. I am afraid I cannot agree here with M.-O. Sweetser: 'Othon . . . a obtenu l'empire dont il était digne . . . La logique de la pièce demandait un dénouement heureux pour la tragédie personnelle comme pour la tragédie politique', *La dramaturgie de Corneille* (Geneva, 1977), p. 218. I would rather adopt, if I dared, the comment of a friend and colleague: that the triumph is a supreme irony – the prize goes to the man who does, and could do, nothing.
18. G. Forestier believes we must suppose that Othon, once out of the palace, masterminds the whole proceedings ('De la politique, ou la stratégie du mensonge dans *Othon*', in *Othon*, ed J. Sanchez, José Feijóo [no place], 1989, pp. LIII–LXXXII; p. LXXIX f.) – which appears improbable given the total lack of initiative he shows before and after.
19. *Héroïsme* II 531–34.

20. *Commentaires* III 921.

Sophonisbe: patriotism and jealousy, pp. 130–34

21. 'Corneille in 1663: the Tragedy of *Sophonisbe*', *PFSCL* XI (1984), No. 21, pp. 575–92.

VI CORNEILLE AFTER CORNEILLE

Agésilas: musical chairs

1. The description comes from R. Brasillach, *Corneille* (1938), pp. 407, 470.
2. 'Curieuse tentative de tragédie, si l'on ose dire, enjoueé et prosaïque' – Stegmann, *Seuil*, p. 686. It certainly lacks the 'poetic' touches of *Attila*.

Attila: a parody?

3. 'Tous les autres historiens [except the one who says his bride killed him] rapportent qu'il avait accoutumé de saigner du nez [which no doubt explains 1599–1604], et que les vapeurs du vin et des viandes dont il se chargea fermèrent le passage à ce sang . . .' (*Au Lecteur*). Copious loss of blood is acceptable in tragedy; Corneille has substituted anger for excess of food and drink (ibid.).
4. Third *Discours*, B 67.
5. First *Discours*, B 6–7.
6. Racine, *Andromaque*, ed. R.C. Knight and H.T. Barnwell (Geneva, 1977), pp. 31 f.
7. *Heraclius*, *Au Lecteur*, B 188.

Suréna: a palinode?

8. *Seuil*, 799.
9. J. Scherer, *La dramaturgie classique en France* (Paris, n.d.), p. 198.
10. Third *Discours*, B 69.

VII CORNEILLE'S IDEAS ON TRAGEDY

1. Lettre 19, to de Pure, *Seuil*, p. 859 f.
2. Barnwell, *Corneille and Racine: an old parallel revisited* (Oxford, 1982), p. 214.
3. *Esquisse d'une histoire de la tragédie française* (Paris, 1927), p. 5.
4. He seems to have regarded the terms *tragique* and *héroïque* as virtual synonyms: '. . . pour m'élever à la dignité du *tragique*, je pris l'appui du grand Sénèque . . . : . . . quand je me suis résolu de repasser du [sic] *heroïque* au naïf, je me suis laissé conduire au fameux Lope de Vega . . .' (*Le Menteur*, epître, *Seuil*, p. 336; my italics).
5. *Traité du Sublime*, tr. Boileau, chap. 1.

6. V. Vedel has used the word and the concept in very nearly the same sense. (*Deux classiques français vus par un étranger*: *Corneille et son temps*, Molière): 'Ce qu'il recherche . . . c'est l'extrême, le paradoxal, tout ce qui s'éloigne le plus possible de la vie bourgeoise et banale. Etonner et déconcerter, voilà, en Italie, le programme esthétique du baroque . . .; pour Corneille aussi c'est là ce qui importe surtout: 'admirer' exprime, dans son langage esthétique, aussi bien l'étonnement que l'admiration' (p. 188 f). 'Ce qu'il cherche dans l'histoire ce sont les records de ce que peut atteindre dans les différentes directions la nature humaine, c'est la limite extrême des oscillations de la vie et des formesparadoxales qu'elle peut emprunter' (p. 191).
7. *Héraclius*, Au lecteur, B 188.
8. *Historiettes* (1960) II, 907, cit. G. Mongrédien, *Recueil des textes relatifs à Corneille* (1972), p. 198.

Index

Characters from plays appear in small capitals (e.g. OTHON). Where references to a play-title and to the title-role coincide, the first set is omitted.